I'M A CELEBRITY ... GET ME OUT OF HERE!

THE INSIDE STORY

MARK BUSK-COWLEY

I'M A CELEBRITY ...
GET ME OUT OF HERE!

THE INSIDE STORY

BANTAM PRESS

LONDON • TORONTO • SYDNEY • AUCKLAND • JOHANNESBURG

CONTENTS

1

WELCOME TO THE JUNGLE

HELLO FROM BRUCEY

G'DAY. MY NAME IS BRUCEY. I'm a cockroach. And this is my story.

It all begins in a jungle in Australia, way back in 2002. There I am: a happy-go-lucky critter without a care in the world. I pass my days nibbling on wallaby droppings and crawling around under a rock.

Looking back now, it seems such a simple life.

I don't know about the big wide world waiting just over the mountains. I've never heard of global superstars like Crissy Rock or Pat Sharp.

You could say I was pretty naïve.

Then one morning I'm sitting there, sucking the guts out of a mouldy toad and watching the sun come up, when I hear the sound of a helicopter approaching. I'm intrigued. Who could it be? Normally helicopters never come this far into the jungle.

The helicopter lands, some people climb out and chuck a net over me, and before I know it I've been stuck in a big barrel with a load of other cockroaches I've never even met.

I don't know what's hit me.

Next thing I know I'm being dumped onto the head of some posh English sheila called Tara Palmer-Tomkinson. She's screaming a proper bluey and jumping around, there's TV cameras everywhere, and off to the side of us there's a couple of funny-looking Geordie lads laughing their heads off.

Bam! That's it. I'm hooked.

And from that day on, show business was the life for me.

It turns out the programme was *I'm A Celebrity … Get Me Out Of Here!* and I'm happy to say it's made me a star. Thirteen series later, I've got my own dressing room, my own stunt double, two thousand wives … and fifty-seven ex-wives.

Since that crazy day back in 2002, I've taken part in more Bushtucker Trials than I care to remember. I've upset more celebrities than Piers Morgan. And I've loved every minute of it.

Now, for the first time, I'm going to tell you my story – the story of *I'm A Celebrity … Get Me Out Of Here!* right from the start. I'll be lifting the lid, spilling the beans, letting the cat out of the bag and throwing the baby out with the bathwater (okay, maybe not that last one).

Over the coming pages, you'll hear from the stars who've called the jungle their home, you'll meet the people behind the scenes who make it all happen and you'll get all the juiciest gossip from thirteen unforgettable series.

It's all in here.

And in the fine tradition of *I'm A Celebrity … Get Me Out Of Here!* there'll also be lots of gratuitous shots of the good-looking campers running around in their underwear.

If you love the show, this is the book for you.

Please buy it. I need the cash. I have alimony problems you wouldn't believe.

This is *I'm A Celebrity … Get Me Out Of Here! – The Inside Story* by me, Brucey the cockroach.

Enjoy!

Brucey

9

2

HOW IT ALL STARTED

'IT'S LIKE GOING ON A CRAP HOLIDAY WITH FIFTEEN PEOPLE YOU NEVER WANT TO SEE AGAIN.'
JOE PASQUALE

I remember during the very first series, I found myself standing in the middle of the camp minutes before the celebrities were due to arrive.

This was something I had spent a year of my life working towards. The first series was about to begin. There was fear, not just because there were a lot of venomous snakes in the jungle surrounding that first camp, but mainly because ITV had invested a huge amount of money in *I'm A Celebrity … Get Me Out Of Here!* Now we had to deliver.

And none of us really knew what was going to happen.

Richard Cowles, Executive Producer and Co-Creator

FOR THOSE OF YOU who don't know, *I'm A Celebrity … Get Me Out Of Here!* is filmed in Australia.

The series normally starts in mid-November, which means that in Australia the weather's changing from warm to hot; while in Britain it's changing from wet to wetter.

The producers have asked me to explain that there are sound technical reasons for filming in Australia: the time difference between Australia and the UK allows them to edit through the night; the rainforest is precisely the kind of brutal, alien environment they need to unsettle the celebrities; the production facilities are second to none and …

Oh come on! Who are they kidding?

We all know they go to Australia because the weather back home sucks, they can walk around in shorts and flip-flops and there are more bars than you can shake a stick at.

I remember when we were looking for that first location. There was Richard [Cowles, Executive Producer], some Aussies, this ex-SAS guy we'd brought over and me. We were wandering around the jungle and we came to a river.

They said, 'How about this spot?'

I looked over and the other side of the river looked much better. So Richard and me jumped in the water with all our clothes on, waded across, climbed out and said, 'Let's do it here.'

Natalka Znak, Executive Producer and Co-Creator

When we were building the set for the first series, there was a creek you had to cross to get to where the camp was. And for the first few months of the set build there was no bridge to get over there.

I lost count of the number of crew members who fell into that creek as they tried to climb over a load of really slippery stones to get to camp.

And that water was freezing.

Alexander Gardiner, Executive Producer series 1–3 and Co-Creator

After the first few days, a load of celebrities came up to the Bush Telegraph to have a right go at me.

They were furious about having to change clothes in front of all the cameras. They demanded more privacy. I wasn't about to build them a dressing room, so I invented what I called a 'modesty smock'. I got Tim from the Art Department to design it. It's basically a sheet with a hole to put your head through.

Turns out it was exactly what they wanted. We've used them ever since and never changed the design.

Richard Cowles, Executive Producer and Co-Creator

THE FIRST SERIES of *I'm A Celebrity … Get Me Out Of Here!* was actually filmed in a place called Mission Beach, near Cairns in Queensland.

The show was on a much smaller scale then. After all, nobody knew how well it would do, or even if it was actually possible. It was just a crazy, wildly ambitious idea some people had come up with, where a bunch of celebs got stuck in a jungle on the other side of the world and they did a live TV show about it every night.

For all ITV knew, it could have sunk like a stone.

This limited budget meant, among other things, that everyone – cast, crew and presenters – stayed in the same place: the Mission Beach Hotel, which, true to its name, was right on the coast.

Imagine the scene: every day hotel staff are faced with the sight of Neil Hamilton lounging around the swimming pool in his shorts, waiting for his wife Christine to get booted out.

Meanwhile, standby celebrity Keith Chegwin is sipping a cola at the bar, praying that someone walks off the show so he can get into the camp. And around him a load of camera operators, producers and editors knock back a few beers at the end of their shift. Every few days another celebrity gets kicked out and checks into the hotel, joining the throng. And when they have the time Ant and Dec pop out of their rooms for a beer as well.

And some days, way out at sea, there's a yacht with a bunch of paparazzi on it, snapping long-lens pictures of it all.

It was a very strange time. Looking back, I can't help but wonder: what is the going rate for a picture of Neil Hamilton with his moobs out? I'm guessing a lot less than a picture of Neil Hamilton with his moobs in.

The downside of everyone living in the same place? There was an outbreak of a nasty tummy bug about halfway through the first series, and because everybody was crammed together, everybody got it. And because it was a live show, nobody could throw a sickie. Which meant there were a load of very ropey-looking camera operators in the studio for a few days. If it hadn't been an open-air studio, it would have smelled like a Bushman's jockstrap in there.

It was great, that first series. Everyone was in it together. None of us really had a clue what we were doing, but we were all determined to make it work.

I remember we'd never worked with Ant and Dec before. So we thought, 'Well, these are two big stars, we'd better treat them properly.'

So we rented them this massive posh mansion. They landed at the airport and I took them over to show them it.

The owners took us on a big tour of the place. They told us the boys would have a cook, a cleaner, all sorts of luxuries. Then they left us alone for a minute and

Ant and Dec looked miserable. I asked them what was up.

They said, 'Can't we come and stay in the hotel with everyone else?' They just wanted to be part of the team. It was that kind of show – big, bold, ambitious – and everyone just wanted to be right there at the heart of it.

So the three of us legged it out of the mansion. And we had a brilliant time with Ant and Dec that year back at the hotel.

Natalka Znak, Executive Producer and Co-Creator

While we were excavating the first site, we came across a pile of bones. We thought they were human. It had us seriously worried – we thought we'd uncovered an ancient Aboriginal graveyard. That would have meant shutting down the whole production and moving to a new location – you can't disturb traditional burial grounds.

While we were working out what to do next, the farmer who owned the land drove up.

'Have you come across the bones yet? I used to breed ostriches and I think I buried the dead ones around here somewhere.'

It turns out it was a pile of ostrich bones. Those legs really looked human.

William 'Fritz' Rogerson, Art Department

We had some crazy arguments when we were putting together that first series. I remember one of the biggest ones was about pants. I was convinced we should only allow people to bring in a single pair of pants each – literally the ones they were wearing. It was meant to be tough, after all. They'd have to wash them every day or go commando.

In the end, after months of discussion, we settled on three pairs each. I still think one pair would have been plenty.

That reminds me of something that happened when Huggy Bear [Antonio Fargas of *Starsky & Hutch* fame] was on the show back in 2004. It was the night before the celebrities go into camp and, as usual, we paid everyone a last visit. I went to see Huggy on my own.

First up, Huggy poured me a huge tumbler of whisky – I'm sure he was just trying to be a good host.

But then he started showing me all the pants he was planning to take in with him. He made this big thing of getting them all out and asking if they were okay. Very odd moment. I had absolutely no idea what to say to him.

Looking back on it now, the conversations we had when we were setting up that first series were hilarious. At one point we were going to ban toilet roll. The celebrities would have had to use leaves. Hilarious.

Natalka Znak, Executive Producer and Co-Creator

I remember we talked about making them forage for food, but it was too risky, because there are things in the jungle that'll poison you in minutes.

Deodorant was banned during the first series. It was all part of the drive to make it completely natural. But the drawback was the celebrities absolutely stank. It was awful. The camera crew were complaining about it, it was that bad. So we allowed deodorant from series 2 onwards, more for our benefit than theirs.

They didn't have a shower in series 1 either. We just told them to wash in the creek.

One of the most important decisions, I think, was about the phone voting. Up until then, all the TV shows were using negative voting – you'd vote for the person you wanted to boot off. But Jo

Scarratt, one of our producers, said we should flip it and use positive voting – meaning you'd vote for the celebrity you wanted to keep in, or who you wanted to face a Bushtucker Trial.

On the bus to site, very close to the show's launch, Jo made this impassioned plea to us, and we finally said, 'Okay, we'll do it your way.' I think that was a masterstroke. On other shows you were losing your strongest characters because people were voting to have a go at them – the Nasty Nick-type baddies. In ours, the really strong characters stayed. It was the ones that disappeared into the background that would get voted off first, which was exactly as it should be.

Natalka Znak, Executive Producer and Co-Creator

We tried to think about absolutely everything when we were creating that first series, but inevitably a couple of details slipped through the net. The biggest one by far was cigarettes. We hadn't given the smokers any thought at all.

Our failure to provide fags goes some way to explaining just how bad-tempered the cast were. Tara Palmer-Tomkinson kept sneaking out of camp in the middle of the night and hassling the camera operators for a smoke.

Alexander Gardiner, Executive Producer series 1–3 and Co-Creator.

3

THE LOCATION

'IT'S LIKE FLYING OVER
A LOAD OF BROCCOLI!'
CRISSY ROCK
(on flying into the jungle)

FOR SERIES 2, the whole kit and caboodle was relocated to a site in a place called Dungay Creek near Queensland's Gold Coast, and the celebrities and their families and friends were put up at the super posh Palazzo Versace hotel in Surfers Paradise. This is where the show has remained ever since.

The change of location meant leaving my family behind. I would have written to them, but I'd left home when I was three days old, and to be honest, I'd forgotten the address.

DUNGAY CREEK ROAD →

← TOURIST DRIVE 42 Murwillumbah

Just six months after the first series, we needed to do an American version of the show for ABC. The truth is, when we were making the first *I'm A Celebrity*, it never occurred to us we'd make another. We thought we were incredibly lucky – and they were incredibly crazy – to let us do it once.

So we never thought beyond that first series. Then, when we got the news they wanted to do the American show, we realized the site we'd used before was literally underwater at that time of year. So we had to look elsewhere, and we found the site in Dungay Creek that we've used ever since.

In the lead-up to the American show there was a massive drought. It was terrible. It didn't rain for months. We had to drill boreholes for water. It was a serious situation. Then, just as the show started, it began to rain and it didn't stop for weeks.

It was miserable.

The Americans didn't recommission it, either. Not for another six years, anyway.

Natalka Znak, Executive Producer and Co-Creator

While the show is on, most of the crew stay in a holiday resort called Coolangatta. It's a surfer's dream, with miles of sandy beaches and great waves.

The crew love those waves. They enjoy looking at them from inside a bar while they're downing beers.

The new site is huge. When the show's in production it's like a small town, teeming with people working in all the areas needed to get the show on air every day.

There's a fleet of vans (in Australia we call them Troopies) that take the crew wherever they need to go on site.

The celebrities are all completely oblivious to this because they're stuck way over in the rainforest.

NOW, HERE'S A REAL TREAT FOR YOU. Over the page, published for the very first time, is a map showing exactly how the site is laid out. This is top-secret information, but I've got a book to sell, so tough luck.

1. The Dressing Rooms

MY DRESSING ROOM is next to Ant and Dec's. It's a little bit smaller, but hey – who's complaining? Well, me, actually. I kicked up a right old stink. But then someone pointed out I'm only two inches long, so by comparison my dressing room is enormous. Which makes me the bigger star.

Of course, I don't do the big 'I am' on set. I'm a regular critter. I don't want special attention because I'm a superstar. I've made that quite clear to my masseuse, my personal chef and the five girls whose job it is to tell me how brilliant I am.

2. Security

ON A SHOW of this scale, security has to be taken very seriously indeed. After all, I don't think it's an exaggeration to say that if something were to happen to me, there would be no *I'm A Celebrity … Get Me Out Of Here!*

Ant and Dec are important as well. But there's two of them. Lose one and it's not the end of the world – that's all I'm saying.

So you won't be surprised to hear that there's a crack security team at the front gate of the site, to stop undesirables from getting in. Okay, so Timmy Mallett slipped through the net, but no system is perfect.

The security team also protects the celebrities around the clock. These guys are extraordinary. In full jungle camouflage gear, they can be literally a few feet outside the camp and nobody suspects a thing.

The security team catches deadly snakes and spiders that could otherwise kill celebrities.

Like I said, no system is perfect.

3. The Catering Tent

THIS IS WHERE the crew gather several times a day to mock the celebrities' plight by ramming mountains of food into their gobs. If you've ever wondered what the word 'gluttony' means, peek into the catering tent at midday and find out. There can be 150 people in here at any one time gorging themselves on free grub.

Meanwhile, less than a kilometre away, some people off the telly are licking the rust off their mess tins and waiting for their next cup of hot water to boil.

It's called irony.

BEEF MUSSAMUM / S

THAI CHICKEN / F
SALAD FRESH COCONUT

GREEN VEG S CURRY
BOK CHOI
VERMICELLI
SALAD N

BRAISED LAMB SHOULDER /

MUSHROOM SOUP CHICKEN STEW

WET LIMA BEAN

PEAS

SPINACH AND RED ONION ALMOND HONEY MUSTARD DRESSING

4. Medical Hut

THIS IS WHERE Medic Bob can be found when he isn't down at the Trials Clearing putting the fear of God into celebrities with one of his reassuring pre-Trial pep talks ('They are dangerous and they will try to bite you').

The celebrities also come straight here immediately after they have been voted off to make sure they've got all their fingers, toes … and marbles.

Here's what Medic Bob and his team had to deal with during the 2013 series:

- 1 crew member suffered severe anaphylactic shock from a tick bite
- 2 crew members contracted tick fever
- more than 100 ticks were removed from various celebrities and crew members
- 22 carpet pythons were relocated, as well as 12 green tree snakes and 11 brown tree snakes
- 1 large very venomous Stephens' banded snake was removed from under a lighting generator after a crew member almost stepped on it
- 14 cases of tonsillitis
- 11 cases of flu
- 20 cases of the common cold
- 30 insect bites
- 30 rashes
- numerous cuts, grazes and bumps
- 2 people needing stitches
- 2 pregnancy announcements

MEDICAL DEPARTMENT
PLEASE KNOCK THEN WAIT THANK YOU

5. The Kraft Van

DURING THE NIGHT, the catering tent shuts. The Kraft van then takes over, feeding the editors, producers and writers working on the late shift to get the show in shape for broadcast.

The Kraft van has a menu written on the side listing the abundance of healthy salads on offer. This gives the crew something to read while they wait for their hamburgers and chips.

> A few years ago, we had an Aussie guy who came in and set up a coffee stall next to the production office. After a few weeks we had to get rid of him because he was coming in and absolutely stuffing his face all day long from the catering van. It was costing us a fortune.
>
> *Helen Kruger-Bratt, Production Executive*

6. Avid Alley

THIS IS WHERE a group of editors gather once a year in their ongoing attempt to break the world fag-smoking record.

In between the frantic puffing, they labour to put together the film clips (known as VTs) for the show. It's an amazing feat, considering that some of the events you lot watch at home literally happened only minutes before.

The thirteen edit suites run around the clock. There are editors working on the main show VTs, the Bushtucker Trial, highlights packages and, of course, ITV2's *I'm A Celebrity … Get Me Out Of Here! NOW!*

If the editors are girls, the edit suite smells pleasantly of perfume and hair products. If the editors are blokes, you tend to keep the door open.

7. Gallery

THE GALLERY is the nerve centre of the show. It's always dark in here, with a bank of monitors at the front showing loads of different camera shots of the camp.

The logging team work around the clock, watching the live action, making notes on all the goings-on and passing those notes to producers, who head off to the edit suites to begin building VTs for the show. When celebrities come to the Bush Telegraph, someone in the gallery is always on hand to talk to them.

When the programme goes live, the gallery takes complete control of proceedings. Every picture. Every sound. Every moment that's beamed back to the UK.

The live show is when the Executive team and Studio Director really earn their stripes. When they arrive here at around 6 a.m. each morning, they only have one thing on their minds: getting their toast order in before everybody else.

8. Bush Telegraph

CELEBRITIES COME to the Bush Telegraph when they have matters to discuss with the production team: creative issues such as 'Where is my agent?', 'Get me my agent!' and the old favourite 'My agent never agreed to this!'

That's the thing about *I'm A Celebrity … Get Me Out Of Here!* The show's been on for over ten years – it's not like the producers are springing a surprise on the campers.

Every celebrity who's considering taking part is sent a pack including a DVD so they know precisely what they're letting themselves in for. They're invited to meetings where the executives tell them just how tough it will be – the executives call it 'The Talk of Doom'.

At these meetings, the celebrity nods and puts on their listening face. 'It's fine,' they think. 'I went camping in the Lake District as a kid. How hard can it be?' The reality only really hits home when they're sitting on a damp log watching a complete stranger chopping up a single wallaby sausage for twelve people. And then it's a little bit late. And that's when they come to the Bush Telegraph.

The Bush Telegraph is also where the celebrities are called to talk about the events of the day.

9. Studio

THE STUDIO FLOOR is where Ant and Dec work their magic.

The studio is effectively a wooden building on stilts, connected to the jungle by a series of suspension bridges.

When the show is on air, this is home to the studio camera crew, Ant and Dec's make-up and wardrobe team, the sound technicians and Andy Milligan, one of the writers, while the other writer, Mark Busk-Cowley, is in the gallery eating toast and keeping an eye on the football scores.

The studio is completely open air. Partly so viewers can appreciate the beautiful view, and partly because the celebrities come here immediately after eviction, and they absolutely reek. Without a stiff breeze passing through, Ant and Dec would choke.

After leaving the studio, the evicted celebrities walk over a bridge rigged with fireworks, fall into the arms of their loved ones, then rush off to eat their body weight in crisps and chocolate.

10. The Waterfall

THIS IS WHERE the celebrities come to shower, often in skimpy bikinis. Cameramen have been known to fight to the death for the right to film here first thing in the morning.

11. The Trials Clearing

THE TRIALS CLEARING is my second home. This is where I do my thing.

I don't want to boast, but I think it's fair to say that over the past ten years I've created telly gold at the Trials Clearing.

Okay, there have been some great Trials that didn't involve me and my fellow critters: Trials that sent celebrities up on a high wire, dangling out of a plane or flying up on a reverse bungee.

They were scary, no doubt. But be honest: the Trials you remember best involve me and my mates crawling all over a celebrity while they scream for their life.

When the live show finishes, Ant, Dec and the studio crew all come and join me at the Trials Clearing. We have a quick chat about what we need, then we await the arrival of whichever poor sap is facing the next Trial.

What you don't get from TV is a sense of just how bad the Trials Clearing smells. The odour comes from all the bug containers. Several days into a series, the stench is overpowering.

Plus the ground is also crawling with all the critters that have been dumped during previous Trials. The bugs tend to just wander aimlessly about the jungle floor for days on end, wondering where to go next.

Unlike me, they don't have a Winnebago to go back to.

But that's showbiz.

12. The Bug-Breeding Area

THIS IS basically Ibiza for critters: the place where a dedicated team produce all the bugs and beasties needed for the show every year.

13. Snake Rock

SNAKE ROCK is the horrible camp that one group of celebrities has to endure before the groups are brought together in the main camp each year. It's basically a muddy circle in the jungle.

By the time the losers leave this place, the main camp looks like paradise.

SNAKE ROCK

'Do you know how Snake Rock got its name? When we were recceing it, we saw a snake asleep on a rock. That's how clever we are.'

Becca Walker, Executive Producer

14. Production Office

WITHOUT THE production office, there would be no *I'm A Celebrity ... Get Me Out Of Here!*

Because this is where the biscuits can be found.

In the production office there are boxes of biscuit multipacks featuring all kinds of flavours, from gypsy creams to coconut crunch and some kind of pink wafer that looks like it should taste of raspberry but doesn't.

It's someone's job to take the biscuits out of the packets and stick them in a plastic tub. People then polish off all the good ones and leave the weird ones to pile up and go soft.

Do not underestimate the importance of the biscuits. In 2010, the powers that be decided that the biscuit budget (probably only a few million dollars) was excessive. They banned the biscuits.

The entire crew went into meltdown. The powers that be then tried to fob the crew off with a cheap brand of rich tea biscuits. It didn't wash.

Finally, the proper biscuits were reinstated and from that moment on, *I'm A Celebrity ... Get Me Out Of Here!* has gone from strength to strength.

The production office is also home to the Programme Executives, the Director, the Production Executives, the Writers, the PAs and the Press Team.

But it's mainly about the biscuits.

15. The Art Department

THE ART DEPARTMENT'S job is to make ideas a reality, no matter how crazy they sound.

Want a giant emu to drop golden eggs from a height of fifty feet? You need the Art Department.

Want to build a giant and hugely expensive fibreglass cave the celebrities won't even bother sleeping in? You need the Art Department.

Want a pair of gigantic rat pants? You need treatment, mate. But in the meantime, the Art Department will sort them out.

The Art Department works on just about every area of production: the Trials, the Dingo Dollar Challenges, the camp, the studio. It's amazing what they can knock up with a hammer, a chisel and a few hours' notice.

16. The Camp

AND HERE IT IS, ladies and gentlemen: the camp.

Home to Olympians, Hollywood legends, world champions, a serving MP, pop stars, punks, some proper princesses and quite a few snakes.

Just down from the camp is the creek, where the celebs can wash their clothes and collect water.

It takes the producers a great deal of time to prepare the camp for each new group of celebrities. It's all about the little luxuries.

They have to make sure there aren't any.

4

THE CRITTERS

'I'LL NEVER FORGET THE
FIRST NIGHT, THERE WAS
A SNAKE UNDER MY BED
SNIFFING MY BOTTOM.'
KERRY KATONA

RIGHT. IT'S TIME to talk about the stars of *I'm A Celebrity … Get Me Out Of Here!* They're small, they're mischievous and they take great pleasure in driving our campers crazy.

No, not Ant and Dec – it's us critters.

You know, me and my mates don't get much credit, but us critters have got the toughest job in the jungle. Day after day, there we are, stuck in coffins scaring celebrities, stuck in helmets scaring celebrities or stuck in caves scaring celebrities.

It might sound like a laugh, but trust me, after those campers have spent a week wading through fish guts, washing in pond water and doing their business in the Dunny, they smell worse than a student's sock drawer.

And hanging out with them – well, on them – is no picnic.

And talking of picnics: let's face it, there aren't many careers where being eaten by some bloke out of *Hollyoaks* is a hazard of the job.

Fellow critters. You make *I'm A Celebrity … Get Me Out Of Here!* what it is. I salute you.

Of course, it isn't just the celebrities that need to look out for critters. Executive Producer Richard Cowles was actually stung on the bum by a scorpion while he was sitting at his desk in his office!

Over the years, members of the crew have suffered snake and spider bites, some of them quite serious.

And in the camp, leeches and paralysis ticks are so commonplace that after a while the celebrities barely even bat an eyebrow.

Being bitten on the bum by a scorpion was a bit of a low point. Not because my life was in any danger, but because my hard-man glory was so short-lived. I'd been sitting at my desk when I felt a searing pain – quite literally a pain in the arse.

When I stood up, a scorpion dropped out of my shorts. I headed off to see Medic Bob and had to bare my bum to him. It was turning into a bad day all round.

For a while, I received all the sympathy and attention I thought I deserved. Unfortunately, a short while later, a security guard who was already head and shoulders above me in the real-man stakes, decided to demonstrate exactly what real men do on such an occasion. He'd been watching the Celebrity Chest that two celebrities were heading towards when he noticed that a highly venomous snake was crawling over it. He decided to move the snake to a safe distance, but after he picked it up, he tripped on a rock and lost his grip. The snake sank its teeth – and a load of venom – into him. But rather than dropping his shorts for Medic Bob and wallowing in the sympathy of all the female producers, he ignored the searing pain, identified the snake, recognized he'd been bitten by one like that before, took the anti-venom and decided to finish his shift (a further four hours) before quietly taking himself off to hospital.

These Aussies are proper hard.

Richard Cowles, Executive Producer and Co-Creator

'AAARGH. OH MY GOD IT WAS ON ME!' CHRISTOPHER BIGGINS

WHEN HE FOUND a tick on his neck after he'd been in the jungle for a week or so, Eric Bristow famously kept smoking his roll-up. It's amazing what a week in that camp can do to a man. The tick didn't get off so easy, though. He had to spend a month in rehab.

'I SAT THERE EVERY NIGHT WITH MY HAND OVER MY MOUTH PRAYING THAT AN ANIMAL WOULDN'T CRAWL INTO IT.'
STACEY SOLOMON

In 2011 we had a major problem. A load of redback spiders attacked the cockroaches we'd been breeding for the show and it was a serious struggle breeding a fresh batch that would be ready for the show going to air.

Helen Kruger-Bratt, Production Executive

In the early days, before we had a big Art Department to make all the props for the show, we really freaked out some of the local shops with our requests.

I remember going into a tailor's in Tully, near the site. I asked the lady behind the counter if she could design and make me a pair of giant critter pants – basically, giant plastic dungarees we could dump bugs in. She looked at me like I was completely crazy.

Alexander Gardiner, Executive Producer series 1–3 and Co-Creator

THE BUG-BREEDING AREA

THESE DAYS *I'm A Celebrity … Get Me Out Of Here!*
has a dedicated bug-breeding factory on site.
Yes, bug-breeding is an actual job.

It's like matchmaking, but a lot less complicated.
Bugs aren't fussy.

The show requires literally hundreds of thousands
of critters during the three-week run. By and large,
once they've been used in a Trial they tend to
wander off into the jungle or just fly away, so you
can't use them twice.

Here's what they bred for series 13:

- 250,000 cockroaches (250,001
    including me)
- 153,000 crickets
- 2.5 million mealworms
- 400 spiders
- 500 rats
- 30 snakes
- 6 1-metre-long crocodiles
- 20 small crocodiles
- And a partridge in a pear tree. Okay, I made that last one up.

The bug-breeding area is one of the quieter places on site, mainly because
it stinks. No kidding. A lot of us critters

breed in poo and rotting stuff, so it can
get pretty ripe on a hot day.

Of course, it's all super efficient now,
but back when the show first started,
the producers had no idea how many
bugs and critters they'd need for the
Bushtucker Trials.

All they knew was they'd need a lot.

MY TOP TEN NASTY MATES

All these NASTY CRITTERS belong in and native to the area around where *I'm A Celebrity... Get Me Out Of Here!* is filmed. Every one of these nasty mates has been found in or near the camp.

1. THE FUNNEL WEB SPIDER

In at number one, it's not even a snake. It's a spider! Funnel webs are small, shiny, black, and mean as hell. Their fangs literally drip with venom.

Funnel webs absolutely refuse to take a chill pill; they're plain cranky. They come looking for trouble, pointing their fangs all over the place and rearing up on their little back legs. They're the animal kingdom's version of those drunk lads you see outside clubs whose girlfriends are always having to hold them back.

Funnel webs show up regularly at the Kraft van, the edit suites, outside the production offices and in camp.

2. ROUGH-SCALED SNAKE

To make extra sure this is a genuine rough-scaled snake, you'd really need to stroke the skin. But by then it will have killed you, so I wouldn't bother.

3. STEPHENS' BANDED SNAKE

Okay, the snake's called Stephen. But don't let the name fool you. He's not a nerd and he will kill you. To make matters worse, he's in a really bad mood about being called Stephen in the first place.

4. BROWN SNAKE
Keep the name simple. It's a snake, it's brown ... brown snake. And yes, this little bugger can kill you.

5. BLACK SNAKE
The brown snake is also available in black. And it will also kill you.

6. SMALL-EYED SNAKE
It has really small eyes. Or maybe it's just squinting. While you're pondering this fact, it will kill you.

7. BROWN TREE SNAKE
The brown tree snake is not considered deadly. His venom will only leave you writhing in agony and foaming at the mouth.

By snake standards, that makes him almost cuddly.

8. GOLDEN-CROWNED SNAKE
Another of the less venomous varieties whose bite can only hurt people. That's not to say this bad boy wouldn't like to kill you, given half a chance.

9. YELLOW-FACED WHIP SNAKE
The yellow-faced whip snake only makes it in at number nine, because he can't kill you. Wimp.

10. AUSTRALIAN CARPET PYTHON
The Australian carpet python is not venomous. He likes to crush his prey to death really slowly, then dislocate his own jaw and eat the victim whole. Then he'll lie around for a few days dissolving the victim in his gastric juices.

The carpet python is not the fastest mover, so you would have to be seriously stupid to get yourself killed by one.

For that reason, and the fact that he dissed me once at a Trial, he's only in at number ten. In your face, carpet python.

'WHEN THE JUNGLE GOES DARK IS WHEN YOU'RE THE SCAREDEST YOU'LL EVER BE. YOU SLEEP IN YOUR SHOES, YOUR SOCKS, YOUR HAT, EVERY PIECE OF CLOTHING YOU CAN THINK OF, AND YOU ZIP YOURSELF UP IN YOUR SLEEPING BAG WITH A LITTLE AIRHOLE.'
KERRY KATONA

I remember arriving in Australia for the first time and being packed off in a car to go and buy some bugs for the dry runs and Trials testing. I arrived at a farm in the middle of nowhere. They sold critters to people with pet spiders or snakes, little packets of them, the size of crisp bags. They asked me how many I wanted. 'Half a million?' They thought I was crazy.

Mark Busk-Cowley, Writer and Co-Creator

'THERE ARE SOME STRANGE LAWS IN AUSTRALIA. WE ACTUALLY NEED A LICENCE TO HAVE A STUFFED KANGAROO ON SET.'
HELEN KRUGER-BRATT, PRODUCTION EXECUTIVE

HOUSE OF FLIES

BACK IN 2004, Brian Harvey took on a Bushtucker Trial called House of Pies. It was proper disgusting – poor old Brian was stuck in a tiny shed full of flies and could only use his mouth to find the stars inside pies. Which meant mouthfuls of flies. The Trial really freaked Brian out. Days later you could see him sitting on his log, swatting away at thin air with this haunted look on his face. Brian was never really the same afterwards, and it wasn't long before he walked out of camp.

I can picture him now, sitting back in his hotel room, thrashing away at clouds of imaginary flies.

The Trial featured a record-breaking one and a half million of the buggers. It took quite a while to breed that lot.

But what viewers didn't know was that because they'd been bred in controlled conditions, most of the flies had absolutely no idea how to actually fly. They just crawled along the table, fell on the floor and wandered about.

You see some pretty weird sights in the jungle.

In 2013, while the cameras were following Rebecca Adlington walking back after completing her Trial, they spotted a python halfway through eating a possum. It was disgusting – the poor possum's back legs were sticking out of the python's mouth. The footage was briefly featured in Rebecca's Trial VT, but we took it out before the show went on air, because it really wasn't pleasant to look at.

Another time that year, I spotted a huntsman spider fighting a stick insect on the bonnet of my car. In the end it took about three hours, but eventually the spider won.

Richard Cowles, Executive Producer and Co-Creator

5

SETTING UP CAMP

'I WOKE UP AND SAW
THIS LITTLE RAT
BOUNCING ABOUT.
AND I REALIZED: OH MY
GOD, I'M IN THE MIDDLE
OF THE JUNGLE.
I WANT MY MUM.'
MARK WRIGHT

PEOPLE ARE OFTEN SURPRISED to hear about the incredible amount of work that goes into producing *I'm A Celebrity … Get Me Out Of Here!* every year. After all, to the casual observer, the camp is little more than a muddy circle with some canvas beds around it and a fire in the middle. Of course, to the trained eye the camp is … okay, it's a muddy circle with some canvas beds around it and a fire in the middle. But that's not the point. The difficulty comes when you want to broadcast what's going on in there to people on the other side of the world, live on TV. To do that means rigging up a bunch of cameras and lights and microphones and wires and all that sort of stuff.

Stop me if I'm getting too technical.

It's a massive operation that takes months of planning. At least that's what they tell me. I'm a massive star, so I don't get involved in any of that nonsense. While all these losers are hard at work putting the set together, I'm chilling with my homies at my beach condo down in Byron Bay.

When the show's in full swing, there's a crew of over 500 people working on site around the clock. That's when I come on board. Every day, I roll up in my limo at the last possible minute, do my thing, then head back to the Winnebago for a deep tissue massage and a glass of pinot noir.

It's exhausting. That masseur gives me such a pummelling, I can tell you.

When work's over for the day, I normally play a quick round of golf with Ant and Dec before heading off for dinner with the guys – Russell Crowe, Hugh Jackman, Cate Blanchett, whoever's in town.

I LOVE BEING FAMOUS.

Here's a few of the incredible facts and figures behind the show.

THE FOOD MOUNTAIN

IT'S A TALE OF TWO very different worlds.

Down in the camp, a load of tired, smelly celebrities are staring at a tiny cup of rice and beans, otherwise known as breakfast, lunch and dinner.

Meanwhile, in the catering tent not too far away, the crew are shovelling food down their gobs like it's going out of fashion.

I swear you'd think these people had never been fed before. It's a proper feeding frenzy. I stay well clear of it – I always have half a feeling someone'll pick me up and shove me in their mouth while they're at it.

Skinny rakes show up to work on this show, and by the time they leave a month later, they've got wobbling love handles and type 2 diabetes.

There's something about a free meal; people lose all judgement.

What the crew ate in 2013

IN TOTAL, THE CREW scoffed about 8,500 meals during the production of *I'm A Celebrity … Get Me Out Of Here!* series 13.

Every day they ploughed through:
- 15kg bacon
- 540 eggs
- 7kg muesli
- 70kg potatoes
- 80kg beef
- 60kg chicken
- 50kg pork
- 20kg fish
- 3kg ham
- 2kg salami
- 4kg burger patties

And not a baked bean in sight.

THE BIG BUILD

KEEPING THE *I'm A Celebrity...Get Me Out Of Here!* site ticking over is a major operation.

There's a limited crew on site 365 days of the year. But things really kick off four months before the show goes on air.

The Art Department and Trials Team get cracking on all the props and sets in August.

The site is massive. I mean proper massive. And linking the production area to the camp is a huge job. It involves:

- half a mile of suspension bridges
- 4 miles of rope
- 5 miles of steel cabling
- 60 tonnes of scaffolding

The suspension bridges are very important. They link the studio to the rainforest, so that Ant and Dec can get into camp every morning to ruin someone's day.

THE SATELLITE DISHES

THERE ARE TWO SATELLITE dishes on site to beam the show around the world. Only one is needed. The other is on standby in case the first one goes down.

If we lose both dishes, ITV has an emergency plan in place. They'll screen a one-hour documentary, *Piers Meets Brucey*, in which Piers Morgan looks back at my incredible rags-to-riches life story.

It's a proper tearjerker. I cry like a baby when Piers asks me about my troubled childhood. You would too if you'd seen your dad eating ten of your brothers.

Every day I pray these dishes will fail so

ICH BIN EIN STAR –
HOLT MICH HIER RAUS!

YOU LOT PROBABLY think my job is easy.

You all reckon I've got three or four weeks of graft from November to December, then I put my feet up for the next eleven months.

Well, you couldn't be more wrong. Because almost immediately after the British crew pack their bags and head back to Pommieland, the Germans arrive.

Yes, the Germans have their own hugely successful version of the show that goes out in January. It's called *Ich Bin Ein Star – Holt Mich Hier Raus!* I'm a big star in Germany. I don't have what you'd call a speaking role, so the language barrier isn't an issue.

And the Germans aren't the only ones to have jumped on board the *I'm A Celebrity* express. Sweden, France, India, Hungary and the USA have all made their own versions of the show.

Thanks to them, I'm a global star. Huge.

Seriously, I can't walk down Sunset Boulevard. It's impossible.

To be fair, I can't walk down any street because I'll get stood on, but you get my point.

GETTING THE CELEBRITIES IN AND OUT OF CAMP

ONE OF THE MOST important jobs in the lead-up to the show every year is getting the celebrities over to Australia and into camp in one piece.

After all, the producers want the stars to arrive fit, raring to go and bursting with optimism.

It makes it so much more fun to watch as their spirits are then brutally crushed.

Here's Casting Executive David Harvey on what happens to the celebrities from the day they leave home to the moment they get dropped back at the airport in Australia, several kilos lighter and a whole lot wiser.

Where possible, members of the production team chaperone the celebrities all the way from the UK to Australia. It's a long flight, so there's plenty of time for the nerves to kick in.

The celebrities can have a drink on the plane, but we've had some people in the past for whom, because of what they're getting into in the jungle, the advice from our medical and psych team is that they should cut down on drinking before they go in, so it's not all such a shock to the system. In some cases we make sure the minibar in their hotel room has been emptied to spare them any temptation.

Once the celebrity is at the hotel, they're in lockdown.

Lockdown means that when they land, they can make one phone call home to say, 'I've got here safely, and I'm fine.' Then we take their phone off them, their laptop, their iPad – so they have no way of communicating with home. Ideally we'd like to put them in a hotel room that doesn't have a phone, but because of fire regulations you can't do that. But as we're paying their bill we can keep an eye on that and make sure they're not making calls.

The thing is, it's only a TV show, and who's to say that if they hand over a laptop or a mobile phone, they don't have another laptop or a load of mobile phones? David Haye had loads of phones – there was a family one, a business one, a sports one ... There were about four or five phones in total, but we got them all – I think.

Right: The Palazzo Versace hotel in Surfers Paradise

I remember Malcolm McLaren managed to give security the slip. He went for a walk on the beach at 3 a.m. to 'see the area' before he went into camp. Or, as it turned out, went home.

While the celebrities are in the hotel, there are various meetings. There's a meeting with the Health and Safety guys. Medic Bob will come and see them. Wardrobe will meet them. Although we've already fitted the celebs with clothes, we'll make sure that what they're going to be wearing is comfortable and do any last-minute alterations. We've found that celebrities often lie about their sizes when we ask them – everybody's a size 10 – so there could well be changes to be made.

The Execs will meet every celeb to go through the rules and just to see how they are. They're not told a huge amount – it's all on a 'need to know' basis.

When Becca [Walker, Executive Producer] and I go round on the Thursday, we'll say to them, 'Okay, filming will start tomorrow,' but we'll just give them the bare essentials, like 'This is what you should wear' and maybe a call time.

They're all in different hotels at this point – scattered all across the Gold Coast – because we don't want them to meet each other. We want them to meet on camera, so they're all in a different hotel, each with a chaperone. Which means that for all these meetings, we have to go to *them*.

On the day they go in, they all meet up at a location – it might be at a swanky villa, or for example in 2013 the first four met on a yacht and tracked the others down on an island.

We do advise them not to stuff their faces before they go in. It's best for them to get their stomachs used to smaller portions. People have ignored that in the past, but I think they're more likely to struggle if they're cramming croissants in their mouths when they have that final breakfast before heading in.

Right: Scott Henshall

The thing is, ultimately they will have to go hungry, and I think it's better if they build themselves up to it.

Once they've gone in, we've then got the late arrivals turning up in Australia – the two celebrities who'll join the camp a few days in. We aim to time the late arrivals landing in Australia so that they can't see the first transmission of the show and ideally when they land and make their phone call home, their friends or family won't have seen the first show go out, so that they can't be told, 'Oh, so-and-so is on the programme and X, Y and Z have happened.'

We want to keep the late arrivals as much in the dark as everyone else is when they go in. So we try to get them into lockdown, at the latest, the night before the first transmission.

Once everybody is in camp, and just before the vote-offs start, the next stage is to get the friends and family out to Australia. We don't necessarily have to stagger those flights – it's okay if they meet. They all stay at the Versace hotel in Surfers Paradise – very posh.

The night before the first vote-off, we hold a drinks reception for all the friends and family where we explain what they'll be doing from that point on.

Usually they have to meet in the lobby at around 5 a.m. It's not too bad because with jet lag they're normally up early anyway. The trip to site takes about an hour and a quarter. Once they arrive, they can grab breakfast down in the social tent and start watching the show as it goes out live.

People do sometimes sleep in, which is a pain, because it holds the bus up. Most of the friends and family are fine – they want to see how their loved ones are getting on.

It tends to be more of an issue once the celebrities have been evicted and they have to go in the next morning for their ITV2 interview. I remember Scott Henshall: he'd been up all night celebrating getting out of the jungle. I remember telling him, 'Your call time will be five. We need to leave here by five thirty.'

He said, 'Yeah, yeah, yeah.' But he was up until at least 4 a.m. We could not get him out of bed. When he was awake, he was a complete zombie. It took forever to get him ready. We missed the start of the show. They normally get there to see how their exit has affected the rest of camp, but he missed all that. Nightmare.

When the celebrities do come out, the first thing they do is see the show's psychiatrist and Medic Bob down in their office. They get a debriefing and Bob will check their weight and blood pressure and so on. Usually they'll have met their loved one at the end of the bridge, but there might be other family members they've not met – like kids who are too small to go up to the bridge.

They go back to the site in a car with a camera crew. They're given a phone to make some calls – to a loved one or their agent.

Normally they'll go and grab a bacon sandwich and some sort of food. Medic Bob does advise them – he recommends they take it easy on the food for the first couple of days. Food is a big issue. Apparently Britt Ekland went to McDonald's the moment she left – there's one next to the Versace, and as soon as she saw it she was in there.

Martina Navratilova saw a roadside stall selling crates of mangoes. She bought a whole crate of mangoes and that's all she wanted to eat.

When they get back to the hotel, we reunite them with their belongings – their luggage, their phone, their laptop. They check it's all there and they sign for it. But their work's still not over.

They have time to have a shower and get changed. Then we'll do a catch-up interview, and there might be requests from *This Morning* and *Daybreak* to do live links. If they've got an exclusive deal, we have to get that in somehow. And if they want to do a press 'round table' then that has to be squeezed in as well. So there's quite a bit to get done by 6.30–7 p.m.

After that, they can enjoy however many days are left until the series ends and they head for home.

David Harvey, Casting Executive

'm A Celebrity … Get Me Out Of Here! is a bit like a runaway train.

We spend three weeks trying to keep it on the rails, before ultimately it screeches to a stop in the final show.

We start each new series with a new bunch of celebrities, brand-new format twists and ever more inventive ways of delivering bugs through the Bushtucker Trials. However, despite the months and months of planning, it's impossible to predict how the show will turn out. We have no idea how the celebrities will respond to jungle life, and often the way they do takes us by surprise. Who knew Helen Flanagan would be quite so terrified of doing any Trial at all, but quite fearless when it came to facing a hungry camp? Or that Gillian McKeith would have the forethought to use her pants to smuggle spices in, but faint at the merest whiff of a bug?

It can get the heart pumping, but it's the sheer unpredictability of the show that makes it so great. For all the forward planning, the reality of how the celebrities respond is always different and often way better than we could ever have expected.

Richard Cowles, Executive Producer and Co-Creator

I had to tell Nadine Dorries that she'd lost the parliamentary whip. Because they go into lockdown when they go into Australia and they haven't got a clue what's going on – they've got no email access, nothing. It all kicked off back home and we decided it would be unfair of us to let her go ahead into the jungle without letting her know she'd been fired. So muggins got the job of informing her of this. She was shocked – her first reaction was, 'Well they can't.' I remember she was in a fluffy white dressing gown on her bed being informed she'd lost the whip. We said to her: it's up to you, we know this is your career – but she made the decision to carry on.

Becca Walker, Executive Producer

6

THE HOSTS

'THERE'S TWO
YABBIES NOW,
AROUND YOUR HEAD.'
DEC

'WHY DON'T YOU JUST
SHUT UP? I'M GOING TO
YABBIE YOU AFTER THIS.'
JANICE DICKINSON

MOST VIEWERS agree that over the years, two stars have singlehandedly made *I'm A Celebrity ... Get Me Out Of Here!* the massive hit show we all know and love.

All I can say is … thank you. It's incredibly flattering, but honestly, Medic Bob and I couldn't have done it without those lovely lads from Newcastle, Ant and Dec.

Ask anyone on the team and they'll tell you that Ant and Dec are the best in the business. It really is impossible to think of the show with any other presenters.

Hardly surprising, then, that when the format was being put together, theirs were the only names on the list.

For me, Ant and Dec are like a pair of incredibly observant fans of the show. They spot all the little details the rest of us miss; they point out the stupid stuff the celebrities get up to; they laugh their socks off at exactly the same stuff we all do.

Once we knew we were definitely doing the show, I decided the only presenters who could make sense of it were Ant and Dec. I didn't know them but I'd seen them on *Saturday Night Takeaway* and they were just brilliant.

I was pretty naïve in those days. I didn't know the politics – the fact that there's a whole big system, a way of going about booking talent on that level.

So me and Richard [Cowles, Executive Producer] just called their agent and booked in a meeting with Ant and Dec. We went along and pitched the show to the two of them.

We said, 'You are the only people on telly who can do this. Without you there's no show.' We were incredibly passionate about it, but they probably thought we were crazy.

I would never have the balls to do that now. We just had no idea of the politics of those things.

But it worked. They got it straight away.

Natalka Znak, Executive Producer and Co-Creator

ANT AND DEC'S DAILY ROUTINE

5.30 a.m.
Make-up and wardrobe.

6 a.m.
Ant and Dec travel to the studio and rehearse the show.

7 a.m. (9 p.m. in the UK)
The live show airs.

2.30 a.m.
Ant and Dec arrive on site. First up, they go and do any voiceover required.

3 a.m.
Ant and Dec sit down with the Executives (Richard Cowles and Sarah Tyekiff), the writers (Andy Milligan and Mark Busk-Cowley), and director Chris Power to talk through the script.

4 a.m.
Ant, Dec and writers Andy and Mark head off to watch all the VTs.

10 a.m.
Ant and Dec head to the Trials Clearing to walk through the Trial.

10.30 a.m.
The Bushtucker Trial is recorded.

Once the Trial is finished, if the boys don't have any other commitments, they're free to go.

They might head off for a round of golf with me, or back to their hotel to chill out.

HAPPY BIRTHDAY TO ANT!

YOU MIGHT not know that Ant's birthday falls on 18 November. This means that he's been in Australia for his birthday every year since 2004 (the first three series weren't filmed in November), thousands of miles from his wife, Lisa.

To make it up to him, the production team always decorate Ant's office for the special day. They drape the room in yards of bunting and tinsel. Just the kind of thing you really want to see when you arrive for work at two thirty in the morning.

Just for fun, every year Andy [Milligan, Scriptwriter] and I like to sneak in a link referring to what the boys have been up to for Ant's birthday. Two words sum up the subject of pretty much every one of those links: 'alcohol' and 'hangover'.

Mark Busk-Cowley, Writer and Co-Creator

7
THE TRIALS

'IT'S THE SICKNESS IN ALL OF US THAT WANTS TO SEE OTHER PEOPLE SUFFER.'
CHRISTOPHER BIGGINS

WHAT CAN I SAY about the Bushtucker Trials?

Well … they're evil, cruel and nasty. And they're also very, very popular with the great British public.

Could these two facts possibly be connected?

As we all know by now, every day one or more of the celebrities must head off to face a Bushtucker Trial to win food for the camp.

At the beginning, the public vote to decide which celebrity that should be, a custom Gillian McKeith, Janice Dickinson, Helen Flanagan and Jan Leeming are painfully aware of.

Regular viewers will know that when the public choose the same person to face the Bushtucker Trial day after day, the other celebrities traditionally rally around and tell them, 'It's not because they don't like you; it's because they want to see more of you.'

It's a tradition we in the cockroach community call lying.

Personally, I love the Bushtucker Trials. It's a nice little earner in the run-up to Christmas for critters like me. So long as you avoid the Eating Trials: being crunched up and swallowed is a tough one to bounce back from, I don't care who you are.

THE LIVE TRIAL

'IN A REGULAR TRIAL, BOB WILL SIT WITH YOU AND SAY, "THERE ARE GOING TO BE THINGS IN THERE THAT BITE YOU, BUT THEY CAN'T KILL YOU." WHEREAS IN A LIVE TRIAL, ALL YOU HEAR IS "BITE", "KILL" AND YOU'RE LIKE, "OH MY GOD! WHAT'S GOING TO HAPPEN TO ME?"'
STACEY SOLOMON

Of course, the one everyone looks forward to most is the Live Trial – well, everyone except the producers of the show, that is. Just hearing the words Live Trial is enough to send that lot into a cold sweat.

And you can't really blame them. After all, covering a live event on TV is unpredictable at the best of times. Add to the mix a semi-starved, sleep-deprived, shell-shocked celebrity and you can basically throw all your forward planning out of the window.

The Live Trials definitely keep Ant and Dec on their toes. They've also shortened the boys' life expectancies by about ten years.

But it's that very sense of potential carnage that makes the Live Trials so irresistibly watchable for the viewers back home.

'DEAN SCREAMED LIKE A GIRL, WHICH IS ALWAYS FUNNY TO SEE.'
MATT WILLIS

The definitive nerve-pulverizing Live Trial came back in 2006 with Dean Gaffney.

I remember it like it was yesterday.

What happens is, Dean's a late arrival on the show. So he's literally just left the big fancy hotel a couple of hours before.

Dean thinks he's on his way into the camp for the first time to meet the other celebrities. So when he stumbles onto the Live Trial set, he's shocked. And when Ant and Dec tell him he's doing the Live Trial there and then, he's stunned.

There's a quick break before it all kicks off.

During that time, what viewers don't see is Dean turning round and throwing up in the bushes.

So, with just moments to go to the Live Trial, you've got a celebrity talking on the great white telephone who doesn't look like he's ending the call any time soon.

On the set, everybody just holds their breath.

Partly it's the tension. Partly it's the smell of the mushrooms on toast Dean had for his breakfast.

Fortunately, Dean pulls himself together just in time to take a trip to the Bush Spa, and the rest is history.

With those Live Trials, you never know quite what's going to happen.

It's a smart plan, and it pays off big style in 2010 when Gillian McKeith is chosen to take on the Live Trial. In the gallery, the news isn't warmly welcomed. If there'd been a swear box, it would have been filled in five seconds flat.

Gillian McKeith. What a character. Even now, several years later, people are asking: how on earth did that woman ever make it into the jungle?

It's a fair question. And it is true that from the moment Gillian arrived in camp, there were serious health concerns. Mainly for Medic Bob.

Because after spending the best part of a week hauling Gillian around the jungle while she sucked on a gas mask and whined about phobias most of us have never even heard of, the poor man was absolutely out on his feet.

And now she's been voted to face the Live Trial.

Let's just say that when it happens, nobody's feeling too optimistic about the next thirty minutes of their lives. If you can imagine the looks people exchanged on the deck of the *Titanic*, you'll get the picture.

So Gillian gets up, walks over to Ant and Dec, and falls flat on her back, out cold. Bob's called into action again, and the boys throw to a break. Millions of viewers are on the edge of their seats.

Millions more have fallen off their seats laughing.

It's classic telly and it's what makes the Live Trials what they are. But you wouldn't want to be working like that every day …

By the way, after Dean Gaffney's Bush Spa classic, ITV bosses asked the producers if they could do a couple more Live Trials in the next series.

'I ALWAYS FOUND THE TRIALS FUN.
EVEN THOUGH IT WAS ABSOLUTELY AWFUL AND
I WAS NERVOUS, IT WAS AN ADRENALIN RUSH.
THE WORST PART IS THE ANTICIPATION.'
CHARLIE BROOKS

The Live Trial is a huge deal for us in the Trials Team. It's probably the most nerve-racking day on the calendar. As it approaches, the pressure builds as we try to nail down every last detail.

Normally Bushtucker Trials are pre-recorded – if something goes wrong, there's a chance to fix it and go again.

If something goes wrong during a Live Trial, that cock-up is going to be seen by about ten million people. None of us wants that.

It was the year of the Horrods Live Trial with Sinitta. One of the challenges she would face involved sitting underneath a giant suitcase. The suitcase would be suspended above her. It was due to open on cue and release a shower of bugs and slime onto Sinitta's head. In order to make it open at the right moment, the case was sealed shut using electromagnets. These magnets work like ordinary magnets; the difference is, you can turn them on and off with a remote control. We'd used this technique before in Trials. It was a tried and trusted bit of kit.

The morning of the Live Trial is spent frantically running around, trying to make sure everything will be ready on time. Loading the critters into drops (in this case the suitcase) has to be done at the last moment for various reasons.

So we did this with just a few minutes to spare, exactly as planned. That was us – we were all set, ready to face the always stressful Live Trial.

Then the unthinkable happened. We had a power cut on set. These blips of power are not uncommon when you're working in the jungle, but this time it was disastrous. During that single brief loss of power the magnets deactivated, causing both sides of the suitcase to fling open and spill all their bug-filled contents onto the floor below.

Everyone looked round at each other for an explanation, but there was no time for talking; we were about to go live to the nation any minute. Me and a couple of others ran onto the set, much to the director's disbelief (he was watching in horror from the gallery, shouting, 'Get out of there! We're about to go live!')

But we ignored him and got in there, scooping up as many of the critters as we could and mopping up the floor, which was covered in the thick stinky green slime that had oozed out of the case.

Luckily for us, we always prepare for the worst and we keep a stash of spare critters standing by. So we reloaded the suitcase, shut it tight and got out seconds before Ant and Dec read the opening link.

I'd be lying if I said I wasn't massively relieved when the rest of the Trial went to plan and the case stayed shut until we turned off the magnets.

We probably got as big a fright as Sinitta that day. You have to love those Live Trials.

Kevin O'Brien, Trials Producer series 9–11

The First Ever Trial

'TARA HAD GONE OUT TO DO SOMETHING – WE DIDN'T KNOW WHY SHE HAD GONE OUT OF THE CAMP – AND SHE CAME BACK AND SAID, "GOOD GRACIOUS, THEY POURED THINGS ALL OVER ME."'
TONY BLACKBURN

BACK WHEN *I'm A Celebrity … Get Me Out Of Here!* started, they had no idea how nasty they could actually make the Bushtucker Trials. Everyone was really worried about scaring the celebrities out of their minds, fragile things that they are.

Looking back, some of the prototype Trials showed how easy things could have been for our campers. For example, one idea that they actually built was a giant jungle jigsaw puzzle. Yes, to earn meals for camp, the terrified celebrity would have to do a large jigsaw with a jungly picture on it!

Luckily, that idea fell by the wayside.

But it was still a battle to make the Trials as scary as they needed to be.

I remember when Tara Palmer-Tomkinson was facing the first ever Bushtucker Trial, Jungle Shower, back in 2002.

As I said in the introduction to the book, me and a load of other cockroaches are about to be dumped on her head. It's all very exciting.

Now, there's a neck brace attached to the tree to hold Tara's head still, so we'll have somewhere soft to land. But the producers decide it's too cruel and remove it.

Of course, what happens then is that Tara ducks out of the way, and most of us cockroaches just fall onto the ground.

We look like a bunch of amateurs.

I'm furious. This is my big break in TV, after all. I have a word with the producers and, rest assured, they never make the same mistake again.

When I'm in a Bushtucker Trial now, I'm right there with the stars, up close and personal, just the way I like it.

And these days we do things to them we would never have dreamed of back in 2002. We stick their heads in helmets and then fill them right up to the brim with critters. Lovely. You can literally smell their fear.

People often ask me if I like my job. And I say to them, 'What's not to like? I get to meet some of the world's most famous people, crawl all over their faces and make them cry.'

Okay, so I got a bit carried away that time I climbed up Fatima Whitbread's nose, but I swear I thought I saw an old friend up there. Turned out it was only a booger, but by that time I'm wedged up her hooter like a fat guy in a phone box.

For me, the game changer with the Trials, and maybe even the show, was when Nigel Benn did that Trial with the snakes in series 1 – Snake Disaster. It was the fourth Trial ever. Up until that point, nobody – not the celebrities or the viewers at home – ever thought that anyone could actually get hurt. They just never thought we'd let that happen.

But then one of the snakes bit Nigel and it drew blood.

Straight away, you could feel the change in the atmosphere. The celebrities in camp simply couldn't believe it. When Nigel walked back in, he was bleeding! The papers back home were writing about this crazy new show.

It wasn't even a bad bite.

What we've learned is that if the snakes are kept in a really cool environment, they're really sleepy and docile. But if they're a bit warmer, they can get very frisky indeed.

And if you want a major reaction, let the celebrity touch a rat before the Trial starts. That's when they go proper crazy.

Natalka Znak, Executive Producer and Co-Creator

THE EATING TRIALS

IT'S HARD TO BELIEVE that until the arrival of the Eating Trials, people didn't give much thought to the gag reflex. But thanks to *I'm A Celebrity … Get Me Out Of Here!* you Brits are now all too familiar with the sound of celebrities playing tug-of-war with their tummies.

The Eating Trials are the ultimate challenge for anyone in that camp. It's all the misery, humiliation and horror they ever imagined possible, boiled down to thirty minutes of hell they'll remember for the rest of their lives.

I think it's fair to say that viewers reckon they could tackle most Bushtucker Trials. After all, however bad it gets, you can always close your eyes and think of something else – sing a little song to keep your spirits up.

'OH MY GOD.
I JUST ATE
A CAMEL PENIS.'
ASHLEY ROBERTS

Sadly, that's just not possible when you've got a mouthful of kangaroo's bottom.

Eating Trials are definitely my favourite, although I make sure to enjoy them from a safe distance. Get too close and I could find myself being picked up, shoved in a gob and skidding towards somebody's digestive tract before I know what's hit me.

Every year, the Trials Team have an absolute ball (no pun intended) with the Eating Trials. For example, when they were putting together 2012's Revolting Rhymes with Nadine Dorries MP and Helen Flanagan, they came up with this gem:

Hot cross bums. Hot cross bums.

One a penny, two a penny,

Hot cross bums.

Pure poetry.

'I'M NOT A FAN OF THE FOOD TRIALS. I LIKE NICE FOOD.'
STACEY SOLOMON

'I'VE GOT A REALLY BAD GAG REFLEX.'
JOE SWASH

BRUCEY'S EATING TRIALS TOP TEN

There are very few animal bits that haven't been feasted on in the jungle. Here's my personal top ten tummy twisters:

1. KANGAROO'S LADY BITS
For years whenever anybody suggested lady's downstairs parts for an eating Trial they were shouted down.

'It's taboo!' 'It's just plain wrong!'
But this is the 21st century – the age of sexual equality, people! So if we can eat a todger, we can sure as hell chow down on a kangaroo's 'noon', as Stacey Solomon described it.
It's the right thing to do. But it doesn't make it any easier to eat…

2. KANGAROO'S ANUS
Do I really need to explain? It's a kangaroo's anus.

3. FISH EYE
It's that popping sound – it gets you every time.

4. KANGAROO'S TESTICLE
This one pops too. What is it with body parts that pop?

5. KANGAROO PENIS
Very, very chewy by all accounts. And dry. Like a cross between chewing gum and a digestive biscuit.

Imagine trying to get that down when you haven't got much spit.

6. WITCHETTY GRUB
I don't think it's a stretch to say that the Eating Trials put witchetty grubs on the map. But are they grateful? Not one bit.

I've said to them, 'Guys – you've only got yourselves to blame. If you don't want people eating you, don't call yourself grub.'

7. BULL'S EYE
The mint-flavoured boiled sweet version of the Bull's Eye is probably preferable.

8. CROCODILE PENIS
Here's a little known fact. Force a crocodile to watch a celebrity eating one of these and you see actual crocodile tears.

9. CRICKETS
These fellas are actually alive when they get eaten. Not sure if that's worse for them, or the person eating them.

Overall, it's probably worse for the crickets.

10. COCKROACHES
I warn them all, believe me. I tell all the cockroaches to read the small print in the contract. But they get overexcited with the whole TV thing and they'll put their hands up for anything.

I mean, how do they think it's going to end?

Two years ago we had a problem. No one wanted to deal with getting rid of all the fish guts used in the show. Because they absolutely stank. In the end, we had to find an independent contractor to come in and suck up all the rotting guts. Oddly enough, the guy who runs the company is called Mr Poo.

Helen Kruger-Bratt, Production Executive

Every year there seems to be something we can't get. One year we had a shortage of spiders. The locals started collecting them for us and we were giving them five dollars per spider!

In 2012, we had a massive cockroach crisis. We breed some ourselves, but we use so many we still have to buy them in. But this year there was a breeding issue across the entire country. The weather was wrong. All our suppliers said even if they had them, they'd have to go to zoos first. We literally had to scrape them from all over the place. We only had about 150,000. Normally we'd have 250,000.

Fortunately for us, Helen Flanagan was a disaster at Trials – wouldn't do them. So we managed to get through the entire series thanks to her. We could recycle them and use them in the next Trial.

In 2013, it was witchetty grubs. At least once in a series a witchetty grub will make an appearance. But once again, seasonal issues meant there was not a witchetty grub to be found in Australia. We normally get our supply from Tasmania – wasn't happening. So we spread our net far and wide. At one point we had calls out to 100 different suppliers – we were worried we'd wind up with millions of them. But not a single person could give us one. For the first series ever, we didn't feature one. In the Eating Trial it was replaced by a cow's udder.

Becca Walker,
Executive Producer

MY PICK OF THE TRIALS

THE PERFECT Bushtucker Trial needs to have just the right mix of terror, misery and screaming. Even now, I still get a huge kick out of seeing someone off the telly gibbering with fear as another pile of critters lands on their face.

Forget your posh period dramas and documentaries. This is what telly was made for.

Of course, everyone's got a list of their own favourite Trials. But everyone isn't writing this book. So here are *my* classic Trials.

If you think I've missed out one of yours, go and write your own book.

Paul Burrell – Hell Holes, series 4

'THIS IS THE GUY THAT WAS SUPPOSED TO BE DIANA'S ROCK. MORE LIKE A BLOODY BIT OF POPCORN.'
JANET STREET-PORTER

'DON'T BITE ME. WHATEVER YOU ARE, DON'T BITE ME.'
PAUL BURRELL

Way back in 2004, Paul Burrell made Hell Holes his own with an incredible, over-the-top, whimpering, gibbering, wild-eyed performance. Nobody who saw Burrell in action will ever forget it.

Actually, just about the only people who didn't see him in action were Ant and Dec. They spent the entire Trial looking the other way to stop themselves laughing too hard.

Kim Woodburn & Katie Price –
Vile Vending, series 9

Being an invertebrate, there's not much that makes me laugh. It's just the way we are.

Mime? No thanks. Sitcoms? Not my cup of tea. Stand-up comics? No idea what you're on about, mate.

But show me a celebrity retching on a testicle and I just go to pieces. Which is why I loved watching Kim Woodburn taking on Katie Price back in Vile Vending. (By the way, isn't Katie Price a dead ringer for that Jordan, the one that was here years ago? Uncanny.)

Listening to Kim trying to force a fish eye down her throat is a moment I'll never forget. It was clearly the most disgusting experience of her entire life, and for a woman who examined the toilets in student flats for her telly show, that's really saying something.

Honestly, if your dog made a noise like that, you'd have it put down.

Fatima Whitbread & Pat Sharp –
Fill Your Face Extreme, series 11

Okay, I'm biased – but for me this was an absolute classic.

In 2011, Pat Sharp and Fatima Whitbread went head to head for the right to stay in the jungle. The Trial involved them placing Perspex containers on their heads, which were then filled with just about every creature under the sun.

This one had everything: tension, drama, and me disappearing up Fatima's nose.

In the edited show it wasn't clear to viewers just how long I spent in Fatima's schnozzle. It was over in seconds.

It seemed like forever to me, though.

I was told later it was only forty minutes, but you kind of lose track of time in those situations.

Kudos to Medic Bob. If it wasn't for him, I'd still be up there now.

I'll tell you a secret. Not a lot of people know this, but it wasn't the cockroach that almost wiped out Fatima when she was taking on Pat Sharp in their head-to-head survival Trial.

We 'stopped down' three times during that Trial while Fatima and Medic Bob tried to flush the little guy out of her nostril.

Each time they thought they'd got him out, Fatima would try to carry on with the Trial, only to be tickled by the little bugger climbing further up her nose. After the second time, I was told to go in and make sure she was okay.

I took Fatima a few steps away from the crew so that I could have a quiet word with her and check she was happy to carry on. We were standing in a pretty dense bit of jungle.

Now, the crew are all told on *I'm A Celebrity* that the number one killer in the Aussie rainforest is not snakes, spiders, tiger leeches or paralysis ticks, but actually falling branches. Yep, whopping great bits of tree falling from great heights are actually a real threat to you in the jungle, and injure more people than anything else.

So there we were, standing in this tiny clearing, with Bob poking around up Fatima's nose, when we hear an almighty crack, and then without warning a massive branch hits the ground. There was no time

to take cover; you can't see these things coming, so we didn't know where to hide.

Crash! Wallop! This massive branch slams down just inches from where Fatima and I are standing. I jumped out of my skin.

But I don't think Fatima even moved. She was in the zone, a proper Olympian.

'What's going on down there, what's happening?' came a panicky voice in my ear. 'Just nearly got wiped out by a falling tree,' I replied. 'Nothing to worry about, we'll have her back in a minute.'

So we walked Fatima back into position,

where Bob eventually got the cockroach out and she carried on with the Trial.

Poor old Pat Sharp. He never really stood a chance, did he?

Kevin O'Brien, Trials Producer series 9–11

THE ULTIMATE TRIALLISTS

Of course, thanks to you lot, some people have spent a whole lot more time at the Trials Clearing than others.

Here are some of the great serial Triallists.

John Fashanu
Series 2 – 6 Trials

'BE STRONG! BE STRONG! BE STRONG! FOCUS! CONTROL! CONTROL!'
JOHN FASHANU

Jan Leeming
Series 6 – 6 Trials

'IF I SHOW MY WEAKNESS, THEY'LL KEEP VOTING FOR ME BECAUSE IT'S LIKE POKING AT A BEAR IN A CAGE'.
JAN LEEMING

Gillian McKeith
series 10 – 7 Trials

'ARGHHHHHHHHHHHHHH. I'M A CELEBRITY … GET ME OUT OF HERE!'
GILLIAN McKEITH

Helen Flanagan
Series 12 – 7 Trials

'I DON'T THINK I CAN DO THIS …'
HELEN FLANAGAN

I loved working on the Trials. It was hard work, but you were right at the heart of the show, and you got to see some truly classic moments playing out before your eyes.

When the show is on air, the team will arrive on site at 4 or 5 a.m. and start prepping for that day's Trial. Most days it's still dark when we get in.

We start rehearsing and keep an eye on the voting so we know as early as possible which celeb is going to get nominated for that day's Trial.

We rehearse every Trial several times before the celebrity does it. I was always one of the first to try out a Trial. Sometimes I volunteered because it looked like fun, and sometimes I had to do it because nobody else would dare try it.

This goes for everything from death-defying high-wire challenges to underground tunnels, being buried alive (in lots of different ways) and eating some of the most ghastly things imaginable (nine times out of ten, that imagination belonged to me).

As a Trials Producer, you were one of the first people to start work on the show in the year. You'd come out to Australia as early as July and immediately start working on new and exciting ways to scare the heebie-jeebies out of celebrities, or simply make them do something terrible.

You have to get in touch with your wicked side to be a Trials Producer, but I'd be lying if I said I didn't enjoy it.

Kevin O'Brien, Trials Producer series 9–11

THE STORY OF A TRIAL – UP TO YOUR NECK IN IT

'HEY, BRUCEY – how do they come up with those horrible Bushtucker Trials?' I hear you ask.

Well, I'm far too busy to find out, so I thought I'd ask Tom Mills from the Trials Team to lift the lid on their twisted little world.

For the first time ever, here's the story of a Bushtucker Trial, all the way from one person's twisted imagination to the moment Matthew Wright and Joey Essex took the Trial on in front of the watching millions.

The idea for the Trial began with me, and I then worked it up with Ben Aston and John Adams [members of the Trials Team]. In the past, we've done a lot of putting celebs in boxes, but actually burying them alive has always been a dream of mine!

I remember talking about the idea a couple of years ago, but we never worked out how we'd actually do it. We'd thought about ideas where we'd put a celeb in a sarcophagus and then fill it up to their neck. It never happened, but I always thought it'd be nice, so I kept the idea on the backburner.

This year, I remembered it again and thought: let's see if we can bury them up to their necks in sand and then add a load of critters. We talked about it and came up with the idea of putting the celebs in an hourglass, which seemed like a good way of dressing this Trial. In a series of meetings, we developed the idea into what, for quite a while, was called 'The Sands of Time'.

The initial ideas were just sketched out by us in biro on notepads.

As we already had the name 'The Sands of Time', it seemed like a good idea to make time an element of the Trial too, so as well as burying them up to their necks, we would make them guess when ten minutes had elapsed from the moment they began to be buried.

For us, the next stage was to make up a set of images in Powerpoint, which we took to show the *I'm A Celebrity* Execs. They liked the idea and gave us the go-ahead to work on it further. So from that point we went into a lot more detail.

We decided to make it a head-to-head Trial, so we knew we'd need two hourglasses. Then, we emailed the ideas over to our designers in the Art Department in Australia so that they could think about it more and consider the practical aspects. They're the ones who need to work out if the Trial can actually be made a reality. Ideally, we like both the Execs and the designers to give us the go-ahead before we travel to Australia, so we know we're not barking up the wrong tree.

THE SANDS OF TIME   (H2H)

The designers did flag up one thing. Sand is a bit of a nightmare as it can create a lot of dust which can get into your mouth. We don't want to do a Trial where contestants have to wear motorbike helmets or masks, because then you can't see their faces. We always put goggles on them, but we don't want much more than that.

The Art Department in Australia don't start building anything until we get here at the start of August. So once 'The Sands of Time' was signed off, we put it aside and worked on getting all the other Trials signed off – we need twenty in total for each series.

When we got out to Australia we talked about 'The Sands of Time' in much more detail with Art, Health and Safety and Rigging. They did more sketches, then they built a prototype which in no way looked like an hourglass – it was basically two big wooden boxes and you could stand in the bottom half, pull a lever and sand dropped down. At that stage, it was purely about working out how the sand would drop down. And that was when the major sand issues began.

We started by using standard builders' sand. First, we put that in the box and pulled the lever, with no one below it – luckily. The sand just fell in almost brick-shaped lumps. Health and Safety said if that had hit someone on the head, it would have given them whiplash from the impact. So builders' sand was out straight away.

At that point, we started to get a bit worried. The Art Department thought we might have to lose the Trial, so we started thinking of back-up plans.

We went to a builders' yard and looked at loads of different kinds of sand. Ray [Pattison, Art Department] suggested what they call gap-fill sand. It's what they put between patio blocks – it's a lot finer than builders' sand and would flow a lot better.

Again, we dropped it without anyone below it, but because it was so fine it had all this – well, we were calling it dust, but it's actually just smaller particles of sand. That would have been a nightmare, because it would have fogged all the Perspex, fogged all the camera lenses – not to mention that the person in there wouldn't be able to breathe after a while.

Chris Elliot from Health and Safety did take part in one of the tests and he had to get out because he couldn't breathe.

At that point we decided sand was out of the question, which is a bit of a problem on a Trial called 'The Sands of Time'. Then Ray suggested that we try looking at grains – different types of grain that are yellow in colour, so we went to a farm shop.

On the floor of this shop I saw some grain, so I asked the owner what it was and he showed us bags of this stuff called French millet, which was perfect. It's really fine, but not fine enough to make dust. It's yellow, so on camera it looks like sand.

We bought a bag of it and took it back to Art. They were quite happy. We then ordered a tonne of it. We did a test and for the first time it actually worked. It flowed down and there was no dust. To be on the safe side, Art came up with an exhaust system just in case there was any dust – pipes connected to the chamber, so when it started flowing it was like air conditioning, sucking out any fine particles.

Once we'd sorted the sand problem, Art went ahead and began ordering all the Perspex they'd need to create the Trial. We do a lot of stuff that involves Perspex and luckily for us there's a local company that makes everything we need. We can make boxes, but if you need weird stuff like this – shapes that are bent and curved – they use all these clever processes where they heat it and bend it. They can make almost any shape we want, within reason. It can take a while and once the order had gone in we waited about a month for the parts to be delivered.

The next issue was where we would put the Trial, as it needed a lot of space. It was a huge, tall structure so we needed a space that would allow us to get up to the top of it and pour the 'sand' etc in. We finally settled on a site near another Trial called 'In Cave Danger'. The moment 'The Sands of Time' was finished, we would strike it and replace it with 'In Cave Danger' later in the series.

Once the location was decided, it was built and painted – red and yellow for the two teams – and then we did more tests using the millet, just to work out how quickly we wanted to pour it. It all worked very well.

By this time, it was 80 per cent there, but we still had fine-tuning to do – getting the gameplay right. Once the two celebs were buried, ten minutes would pass and we needed a way for them to indicate when they thought the ten minutes were up. We didn't want them just shouting it out – we needed a clear indicator. So we put a button in the container so they had to pull their arm out and press it to light up a sign that said 'TIME UP'.

However, in all these Trials you need to be prepared – particularly in a head-to-head, when you've got quite nervous celebs. If someone bails out straight away, what happens then? If celeb A quits after ten seconds, what do you do? So we made it a rule that the other celebrity would have to carry on in order to win the food.

Finally, after all that work, 'Up To Your Neck In It' (as it was finally called) was signed off and ready to go. In the end, Matthew Wright took on Joey Essex in it. Joey won but, for us, the main thing was it all worked out pretty well.

Tom Mills, Trials Team

8

FOOD

'BAKED BEANS
IS NO GOOD TO
MAN OR BEAST.'
ERIC BRISTOW

RICE AND BEANS isn't everybody's idea of a tasty meal. Actually, rice and beans isn't anybody's idea of a good meal.

But unless someone's bringing home the bacon by winning stars at a Bushtucker Trial, the celebrities had better learn to get used to it.

All of which means that for the campers, food, or the lack of it, is one of the toughest struggles they'll face in the jungle.

Mind you, it's not only them that suffer. I remember one time I'm chilling out by the campfire after a long night's work. I've just spent hours scaring the pants off Rosemary Shrager and a funny-looking fella called Limahl.

Suddenly, I hear a noise like a koala being put through a juicer. I nearly jump out of my skin. Turns out it's only Eric Bristow's stomach rumbling. I swear it was the worst noise I'd ever heard … until the night Limahl sang 'The NeverEnding Story' a capella.

Of course, hunger's never an issue for me because I love my grub – a big fat witchetty grub, like the ones you get in rotting tree stumps. Lovely.

The thing about food is that the celebrities are surprisingly smart when they have to be. And to their credit, over the years they've shown that a little creativity can go a long way.

THE JUNGLE CHEFS
John Burton Race

Back in 2007, chef John Burton Race made delicious feasts out of ingredients such as crocodile, camel and possum. Well, the celebrities said they were delicious – but let's face it, after two weeks of rice, beans and the occasional testicle, licking a stamp is going to taste like dinner at the Ritz.

John's cooking was one of his main contributions to camp life. The other was verbally abusing Lynne Franks.

Gino D'Acampo

King of the Jungle Gino D'Acampo famously made a rat stew. Actually, the less said about that the better.

But like John, Gino's inventiveness in the kitchen made life a whole lot better for the campers.

Rosemary Shrager

In 2012, after Helen Flanagan's performances in the Bushtucker Trials, Rosemary Shrager did an amazing job night after night, transforming rice and water into boiled rice and water.

And talking of the camp of 2012, you know, thanks to Helen, those guys really did go through hell. They ate nothing more than rice and beans for over a week! They had stomach cramps, they had no energy, they suffered severe constipation … it was nasty. At one point the producers were really starting to worry. After all, there's only so much rice in Australia – they nearly had to send out for more.

In 2013, the celebrities won so many stars – I don't think there was a single Trial where they didn't win something – that for the first time ever we actually ran out of Bushtucker food to give them.

At the beginning of the series we stock up on a load of Bushtucker food, and then we work out what to give them on a daily basis, depending on how they do in the Trials, how many stars they win. They went through the lot.

We had to do an emergency run to pick up more Bushtucker food from our suppliers.

Becca Walker, Executive Producer

THE FLYING FOX

The Flying Fox is a real fixture of jungle life. It's a device worked by a system of ropes and pulleys which the producers use to drop food into camp.

Now, over the years, many people have asked me why they use the Flying Fox to send in dinner, rather than simply delivering it by hand.

The answer is quite simple. When the celebrities get a look at what's on the menu, chances are they'd beat the person delivering it to death.

It's a lot safer just to load it into the Flying Fox and drop it in.

HOW TO COOK AN AUTHENTIC JUNGLE MEAL

You will need:
1 chicken
pinch salt
1 red pepper
sprig rosemary
2 onions
1 clove garlic
1 cup beans
1 cup rice

Take the chicken, salt, red pepper, rosemary, onions and garlic and place them in the bin – you did very badly at the Trial, so you didn't win them. Boil the beans and rice in water for ten minutes. Taste the boiled rice and beans. Cry.

THE FOOD RIOT

A decent chef can work their magic on almost any ingredients.

And Antony Worrall Thompson proved just that back in 2003, by taking nine sausages and making a right meal of them.

It was the night of the food ration mutiny.

What happens is, earlier that day John Fashanu has won nine meals in a Bushtucker Trial. So that evening the camp receive nine sausages for their dinner. Antony isn't at all happy, and that's it – off they storm, marching towards the studio in a fully fledged food riot. They stomp over the bridges, with a load of cameras following along.

The show's executive producers, Richard Cowles and Natalka Znak, meet the rebel celebrities on the bridge.

Antony's wielding a sausage, and anyone can tell he's prepared to use it.

Fortunately, Richard and Natalka are both highly skilled in dealing with sausage-wielding TV chefs – it's all part of basic telly training – so they're able to talk Antony down.

But it was a terrifying experience for them both.

'NINE PIECES OF CAULIFLOWER, TWENTY-SEVEN MANGE TOUT, TWO MUSHROOMS AND FOUR KIWI FRUIT AND SOME NUTS WITHOUT A NUT CRACKER. WHAT'S WRONG WITH YOU? IT'S MEANT TO BE NINE MAIN MEALS! IT'S LESS THAN 1,000 CALORIES A DAY!'
ANTONY WORRALL THOMPSON

Even now, years later, I wake up soaked with sweat. It's always the same dream. I'm standing on the bridge and suddenly I've got this smelly, wobbly, meaty little thing right in my face. And he's holding a sausage.

Richard Cowles, Executive Producer and Co-Creator

Richard and I were watching everything on screen up at the production office. Then suddenly they just walked out of camp. We started running down towards the studio and the bridges. I was shouting, 'We've got to stop them.' I made sure we were mic'd up and there was a camera with us, and we went to head them off at the bridge. You don't want them to get all the way out, because that would break the spell for them – once they've seen the outside world again, it wouldn't be the same in the jungle. I just remember Antony Worrall Thompson shouting about sausages.

Half of the celebrities looked really angry. The rest of them looked a bit embarrassed.

The thing is, Antony kind of lost the support of the rest of them. They were annoyed, but he was way over the top. So it just kind of fizzled out.

Natalka Znak, Executive Producer and Co-Creator

THE CALORIE COUNT

As fans of the show will know, food is always an issue in *I'm A Celebrity … Get Me Out Of Here!*

And it's true that there isn't much in the way of tasty grub to go around – virtually none in series when the person doing most of the Bushtucker Trials isn't delivering the goods.

But as much as the lack of actual food is a problem, what's more of a problem is the lack of anything else for the campers to think about. What happens is, after the celebs have been in the jungle for a while, the fear diminishes. And once the fear goes, it's replaced with a crushing, interminable sense of boredom. The days seem to go on forever. There are no distractions. There's absolutely nothing to do.

The only breaks in this endless monotony are breakfast, lunch and dinner. Which makes breakfast, lunch and dinner quite a big deal. Which in turn means that when breakfast, lunch and dinner turn out to be a bowl of rice and beans, the celebrities are going to get a little bit cross.

The truth is that the producers would never let the celebrities actually starve. Years ago, the programme's medical team worked out precisely how many calories a day each celebrity needs in order not to waste away while they're in the camp.

They're nice like that.

JUNGLE ROMANCES

'I LOVE HIM …IF HE WAS
A BIRD, I THINK I'D BE
ALL OVER HIM.'
JOE SWASH
(ON GEORGE TAKEI)

FROM THE VERY FIRST SERIES, the jungle has been a seething hotbed of romantic intrigue. It's hardly surprising when you think about it. You're a long way from home, it's hot, it's sweaty … and there's not a telly in sight. No *telly*, people!

I mean, what else are you going to do?

Personally, I spend *my* spare time making little balls out of poo and rolling them around until they get bigger and bigger. The days just fly by. But celebrities have always been a bit sniffy about that sort of thing … except for Joe Swash.

And what better place to fall in love than a smelly camp in the middle of a rainforest, in front of a hundred cameras and millions of TV viewers? Now *there's* a story for the grandkids! And you don't even have to tell them all the saucy details – just stick on the DVD!

I love a bit of jungle romance. Over the years I've come to recognize that certain twinkle in a celebrity's eye – the one that says, 'Okay, so I've got a girlfriend back home, and this really isn't the time or the place. But you look hot in that red fleece, so what the hell …'

Makes me feel all warm inside.

And you know, it's not just the celebrities who get a bit frisky when we're making the show. I can get pretty lively myself. I think it's the adrenalin rush that comes with doing live telly. For example, back in 2012, I remember falling head over heels for a saucy giant burrowing cockroach called Ella. That girl had legs to die for. Six of them.

I thought Ella was the one, but one night she went to have a rummage around Rosemary Shrager's bra. Rosemary turned over in her sleep and Ella was never seen again. Broke my heart.

Here's a look back at some of the legendary romances from the *I'm A Celebrity … Get Me Out Of Here!* history books.

DARREN DAY & TARA PALMER-TOMKINSON, series 1

WAY BACK IN 2002, Tara and Darren were *I'm A Celebrity … Get Me Out Of Here!*'s original lovebirds. Together, the pair of them wrote the rulebook on jungle romance.

'I THINK THERE WAS SEXUAL TENSION BETWEEN US IF I'M COMPLETELY HONEST.'
DARREN DAY

'IN THE BEGINNING DARREN WAS GREAT. HE'S CUTE-LOOKING – HE'S REALLY ENTERTAINING. WE IMMEDIATELY FORMED A SORT OF BROTHER-SISTER FLIRTATION.'
TARA PALMER-TOMKINSON

'IT WAS BEGINNING TO SMELL QUITE BAD FROM MY POINT OF VIEW … IT REALLY PUT ME OFF HIM.'
TARA PALMER-TOMKINSON

'TARA, I KNOW, HAD A REAL PROBLEM WITH THE FARTING.'
DARREN DAY

DARREN AND TARA'S was the classic boy-meets-girl story, with a jungle twist: first there's the casual flirting, then come the long walks into the rainforest, the stolen glances across the campfire and the snuggles in bed.

Then come the fallouts, the tiffs … and the farts.

They never shared so much as a kiss, but Darren and Tara weren't fooling anyone. Before his trouser trumpets turned things sour, this was true lust.

And it turned out the flirting began before Darren and Tara had even left the hotel to head for the jungle. There were rumours of love notes being passed from room to room – rumours Tara always denied.

Of course, Darren and Tara only had the chance to get up to all that pre-show mischief because in series 1 the celebrities spent a few days at the hotel together before they headed for camp.

From series 2 onwards, the cast were only allowed to meet moments before setting off for the jungle. Why? Because the producers are determined to get every last juicy moment on camera. There's no point in something happening if you, the viewers, don't get to see it.

Anyway, like the smell of one of Darren's bean-fuelled bottom burps, Tara and Darren's romance was short-lived, but lived very, very long in the memory.

PETER ANDRE & KATIE PRICE (JORDAN), series 3

PETER ANDRE: Why don't you forget what they say and do what you want to do?

KATIE PRICE: What do you want to do?

PETER ANDRE: Let's f**k. No, just joking.

KATIE PRICE: Peter, you've already told me you've only got an acorn, it's not even worth going there.

HE WAS THE HANDSOME AUSSIE pop star. She was the innocent English maiden.

And together they made music. Not sweet music, let's be honest – I mean, have you *heard* 'Insania'?

But what a love story it was: two complete strangers, from opposite sides of the world, thrown together by the fickle finger of a television casting executive. And from the moment Peter Andre and Katie Price arrived in camp back in 2003, a mysterious and magical force seemed to draw them together.

Maybe it was the isolation. Maybe it was the jungle's mystical powers. Maybe it was the sound of John Lydon's F-bombs wafting softly up from the creek.

Peter and Katie Price fell for each other hard. I was there, so I saw it for myself. Any fool could tell this was a love that would never, ever die.

I sometimes wonder what happened to the pair of them after they left Australia. Knowing them both as I did, knowing how deep and genuine their love was, I'm betting they went home, had a quiet wedding and headed off together arm in arm, to live happily ever after far from the public's gaze.

Sometimes you just know these things.

CERYS MATTHEWS & MARC BANNERMAN, series 7

'SO WHEN'S YOUR GIRLFRIEND FLYING OUT THEN? SHE'S GOT TO BE HERE TOMORROW, HASN'T SHE?'
JOHN BURTON RACE TO MARC BANNERMAN

MARC BANNERMAN and Cerys Matthews. Nobody imagined them getting together. Least of all Marc's girlfriend. But get together they did.

It took a while, and the nation watched gripped night after night as the romance slowly came to the boil.

Of course, with Marc's girlfriend winging her way to Australia, Marc knew this was your classic dangerous liaison. There was always a small chance one of the hundred cameras pointed at them would spot what was going on.

Cerys and Marc tried to play their cards close to their chests. Sometimes he would cover his microphone and whisper into her ear. I'm not sure this strategy was very effective. One look at Cerys's face and every red-blooded male in the country knew exactly what Marc was asking her.

The relationship lasted three weeks after they got back home, which is pretty good going for a holiday romance.

GEORGE HAMILTON & KIM WOODBURN, series 9

'I USED TO WATCH ALL THOSE OLD CAVALRY FILMS AND I THOUGHT, "DO YOU KNOW, YOU'RE VERY LOVELY, AREN'T YOU, YOU BEAST YOU? I THOUGHT TO MYSELF, IF I WASN'T MARRIED I'D JUMP ON YOU, MATE.'
KIM WOODBURN

OF COURSE, it isn't only the youngsters who get a bit hot under the collar in the steamy heat of the rainforest.

In 2009, golden oldies Kim Woodburn and George Hamilton had their very own jungle affair.

Well, okay, you could argue the attraction was mostly one-way traffic. But who could blame Kim if it was? After all, imagine finding yourself on a camping trip with the movie star you've fancied all your life? You'd think all your Christmases had come at once.

Kim couldn't take her eyes off George. George couldn't believe his luck. Because, after a lifetime of bedding the world's most beautiful women, that man knows every trick in the book. The Hollywood legend played along just enough to have Kim dancing to his tune.

His bed was made. His collar was turned down. His pants were hung up to dry. It was the perfect arrangement for them both.

'I CAN FANTASIZE WHAT IT WOULD BE LIKE TO BE MARRIED TO HER AND COME HOME LATE FROM THE PUB. THAT WOULD NOT BE A GOOD EVENING.'
GEORGE HAMILTON

BROMANCE

'I'M TOTALLY IN LOVE WITH YOU RIGHT NOW… THIS IS WAY BETTER THAN SEX.'
DOUGIE POYNTER
(TO MARK WRIGHT)

WOMEN ARE GREAT. I love them. I've married several thousand, and I'll marry several thousand more.

But let's be honest, lads. They're not the be all and end all. When the chips are down, what a bloke needs more than anything else is his mates.

The jungle has proved this time and time again.

Because for every romance we've seen, there's been a bromance to match. Jungle bromances are basically the same as jungle romances, except for the sloppy kissing.

The bromances have a lot more.

JOE SWASH & GEORGE TAKEI, series 8

IN 2008, JOE SWASH and George Takei gave us possibly the greatest bromance of them all.

They came from two very different worlds: the lieutenant from the *Starship Enterprise* and Mickey, that ginger bloke from Albert Square. Yet this was a match made in heaven, and from the moment they met, Joe Swash and George Takei only had eyes for each other.

They kissed. They cuddled. They made each other laugh. And they never bickered once.

Most couples would kill for the relationship they had.

They even had their own song:

> Olly olly olly
> T**s in the trolley
> B***s in the biscuit tin.
> Sitting in the grass
> Finger up your a**e
> Playing with your ding-a-ling-ling.

So very, very romantic.

Joe returns to the jungle every year to present the ITV2 show *I'm A Celebrity … Get Me Out Of Here! NOW!*

But deep down, you know that for him the jungle's never been quite the same without his Georgey.

MARK WRIGHT & DOUGIE POYNTER, series 11

THIS WASN'T JUST a bromance. This was a bromance love triangle.

At first, Mark Wright only had eyes for Antony Cotton. But once Mark and Dougie got together, Antony was elbowed out of the picture sharpish, and from that moment on, Mark and Dougie were inseparable.

The two of them hung out on their camp beds, gazing into each other's eyes. They whispered sweet nothings to each other.

To top it all, because they were the final two celebrities, they had the chance to spend one very special night together, alone in the jungle.

And boy, did they make the most of it.

It was the perfect bromantic date. No women, loads of fast food and the chance to talk rubbish for hours on end. Bliss.

'I DON'T THINK THERE'S ONE PARTICULAR MOMENT WHEN PEOPLE FELL IN LOVE WITH DOUGIE – I THINK YOU FALL IN LOVE WITH DOUGIE AS SOON AS YOU SEE HIM.'
MARK WRIGHT

'THAT WAS PROBABLY THE MOST ROMANTIC MEAL I'VE EVER HAD.'
DOUGIE POYNTER

KIOSK

IN 2013, a new star was born. A khaki-clad specimen of moustachioed Aussie manhood known only as Kiosk Keith – so named because he has a kiosk and his name is Keith. Keith and his Outback Shack featured in our 2012 series, but he's what you might call a slow burner, and it took until 2013 for the public to truly fall for his uniquely Australian charms.

Anyway, I've been told by the producers to give Keith the chance to send a message to all his fans back in Pommieland. So I head down to the Outback Shack for a chat:

'Hello, Keith. You're a massive star in the UK and people really want to hear what you've got to say for yourself. Your witty observations, your unique take on life, that kind of thing. We're giving you your very own page in this book I'm writing. What do you think of that?'

I think he's thrilled, but it's hard to be sure because Keith slams down the shutter in my face around the time I say 'hello'.

Good old Keith.

KEITH

VINCENT
09020 44 24 **12**

KI

Here's a few interesting facts about Keith:

• Keith's a Capricorn.
• Keith was abandoned shortly after birth and raised in the wild by dingoes. As a result, he's not fully house trained, as I discovered to my cost at a recent drinks do in my Winnebago.
• Keith's the only member of the crew to be registered as an endangered species.
• The reason for Keith's less-than-cheery demeanour is that the Outback Shack has no customers for eleven months of the year. Add to that the fact that Keith only accepts a made-up currency called Dingo Dollars and you can see why business is less than brisk.
• Keith is currently offering 2 for 1 on a range of vegetables.

10

THE SHOWER SCENE

EVERY YEAR YOU GET A REALLY SEXY YOUNGER FEMALE WHO BRINGS ALONG A SPECIAL LITTLE BIKINI FOR THE OLD WATERFALL.

JOE SWASH

OKAY, READERS. I think the time has come to talk about personal hygiene. Not yours, don't panic – I'm sure you're squeaky clean. And not mine – I actually live in dung, so personal hygiene is not something I get too worked up about.

I'm talking about the celebrities.

Yes, if you're hanging around a big, hot, sweaty, dirty camp for weeks on end and you don't want to smell like a Bushman's jockstrap, there's no getting away from it.

You've got to wash.

Fortunately for the celebrities, there's a waterfall just outside the camp, on a rock face above the creek.

Fortunately for you lot, the producers have pointed a whole load of cameras at it.

So every year, some of TV's sexiest stars have the chance to show off their incredible bodies, while earning themselves a bit of spare cash by promoting a hot new lingerie line (yes, Myleene, Ashley and the rest of you, we know exactly what you're up to).

Then an editor spends the night getting all hot and bothered as he puts together a saucy VT, packed with slow-motion shots and soft-focus effects, all played out to a sexy Barry White track.

That's the beauty of *I'm A Celebrity … Get Me Out Of Here!* It's the only show on telly where one minute you could be watching Nadine Dorries MP munching a camel's toe, and the next minute get treated to the sight of Ashley Roberts taking a shower.

It's all about variety.

Anyway, I'm going to shut up at this point – after all, a picture says a thousand words.

Before we go on though, there's one more thing I'd like to add …

OI!!! YOU LOT IN THE BOOKSHOP WHO'VE JUST SKIPPED STRAIGHT TO THIS PAGE FOR A SNEAKY PEEK AT SOME SAUCY PICTURES!!! BUY THE BOOK, YOU CHEAPSKATES!!! I'VE GOT LARVAE TO FEED!!!

Okay, enough from me.

I'm guessing what you lot are wanting is a bit of this …

A load of this …

'IT'S HARD TO HAVE A PROPER WASH THROUGH A SWIMMING TRUNK. YOU KNOW, YOU REALLY WANT TO GIVE THE UNDERCARRIAGE A GOOD SCRUBBING. AND THE BEST WAY TO DO THAT IS GET DOWN TO THE BUFF.'
DAVID HAYE

And a whole
lot of this …

And there's even some
special cases out there
that wouldn't mind an
eyeful of this …
    You sickos!

And as a treat for our older fans, how
about a bit of this …
    I'll tell you something. That David Haye
is so hot he got my temperature soaring.
And he isn't even my species!

CELEBRITY CHEST

Looking at that Myleene picture again reminds me of something …
Now, the producers of *I'm A Celebrity … Get Me Out Of Here!*
aren't completely daft, and when the opportunity arises, they're
more than happy to rise to the occasion.

So, back in 2006, the Celebrity
Chest team get wind of the fact
that Myleene Klass is going to be
taking on the next Chest, along
with Jason Donovan.

That's all the motivation they
need. They work long into the
night, and by sunrise they've
created the perfect challenge – a
Celebrity Chest designed to make
the most of Myleene and Jason's
involvement.

Step one is to get Donovan out of the picture. So they rig up a giant net to whip
him into the air. It works and – WHOOSH!!! – Donovan's history, stuck up in the trees.
Step two: create a situation in which Myleene has to strip off and
take a shower in her bikini. And how do they
do that? By telling Myleene
that she has to release
a key to get Donovan
down, but the key is
stuck in a bar of soap,
so the only way to free
it is by rubbing the soap
all over her soaking
body.

Genius.

It only goes to show: people are at their most creative when they're motivated.

Okay, readers, you've seen the rest; now prepare for the best.

Waiting for you on the next page, ladies and gentlemen, is a treat that I think you'll agree, justifies the price of this book on its own.

If you're pregnant, suffering from heart problems, or you're of a nervous disposition, you may want to think seriously about whether you can handle the sheer animal sexuality you're about to behold.

I leave that decision down to you.

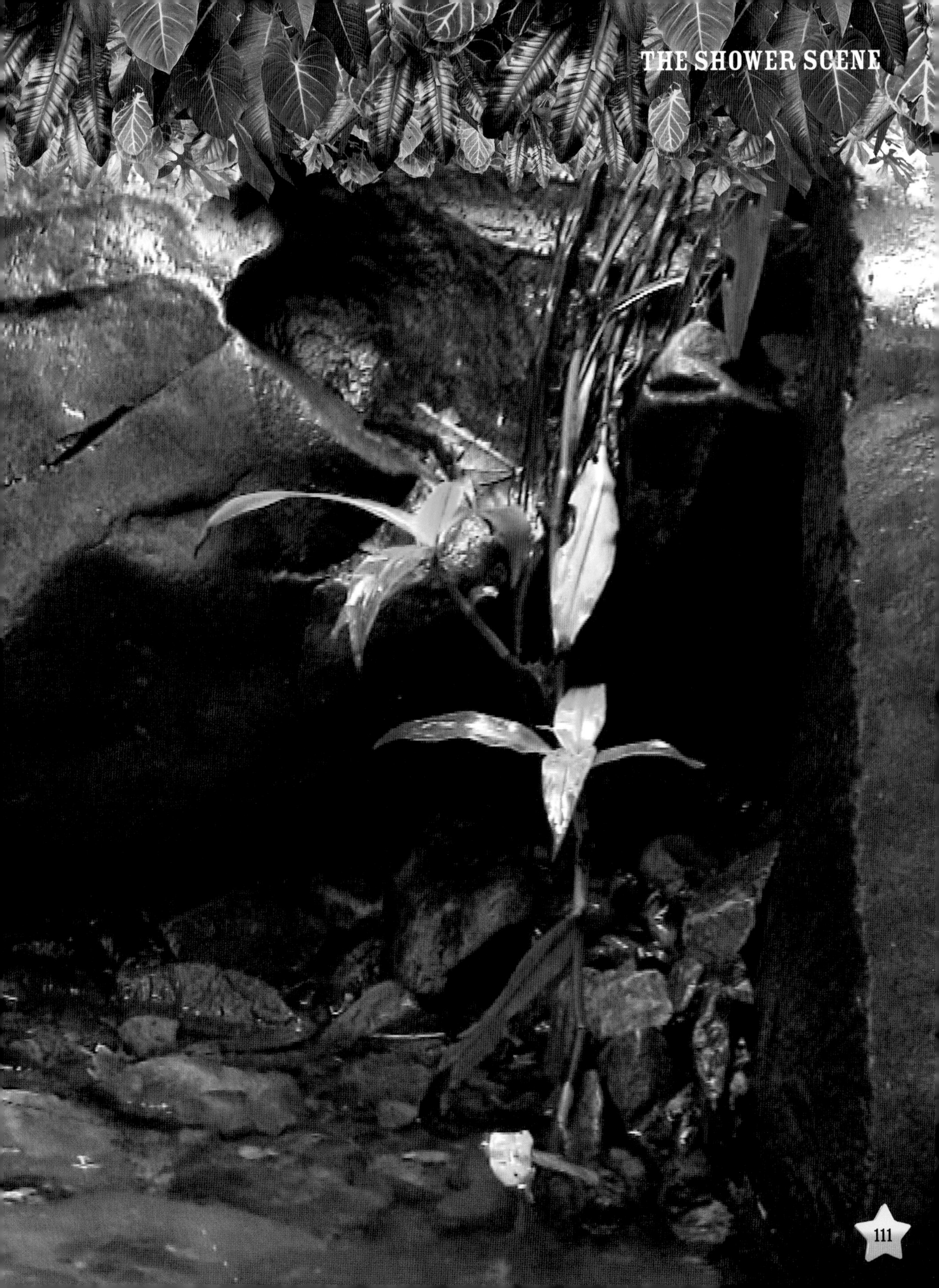

11

THE FIGHTS AND THE FEUDS

'WHEN WE WERE ALL AT THE HOTEL ABOUT TO GO IN, EVERYBODY WAS ROWING EVEN THEN!'
TONY BLACKBURN

WE'VE BEEN making *I'm A Celebrity … Get Me Out Of Here!* for a while now. And that means there are some things we know are pretty much guaranteed to happen every year, with each new bunch of celebrities, no matter what.

And one of these is a little process we like to call…

THE DAY 4 FALLOUT

It's not an exact science – it varies by a day or so from year to year – but more often than not this is what happens.

Day 1

The brand-new celebrities arrive in the jungle. They're all a bit scared. And they're all on their best behaviour. Mainly because they've got their families' last, desperate words ringing in their ears:

'Dear God, please keep that temper of yours in check. And don't be yourself! Act like a normal person!!!'

So on that first day, it's all smiles.

This is a popularity contest, after all.

Day 2

They made it to the jungle! And they survived the first night!

They're so overjoyed to discover nothing ate them while they slept that they're filled with love for their fellow campers.

'We can do this! I really think we can do this! If we all just stick together …'

Plus, everywhere they turn there's cameras pointing at them, and they want to show the world what fun guys they are.

This is a popularity contest, after all.

Day 3

By Day 3, they're on the brink.

'Rice and beans! Rice and beans! All I've had to eat for days now is rice and beans.' All because so-and-so couldn't face a Bushtucker Trial.'

But they can still hear the voices echoing in their head:

'Watch that temper! Pleeeeasssse!'

And those cameras. Those damn cameras are everywhere. Smile, dammit. Smile.

This is a stupid popularity contest, after all.

Day 4

Around about Day 4 is when it tends to kick off.

'Give me some food. I hate you all. And you can take that camera and your popularity contest and shove it up your–'

You get the idea.

Yes, every year the celebrities head for camp with the best intentions: they'll smile come what may; they'll get along with their campmates no matter what. No one's going to see their dark side.

But about four days in, something gives.

The hunger really kicks in, they've gone through a detox that would make the Priory shudder, and they're beyond caring about those cameras.

That, my friends, is when the fighting starts.

> 'WE'VE ALL GOT A DARK SIDE OF OUR PERSONALITY. BUT WHY DO YOU WANT TO EXPOSE THAT IN FRONT OF 13 MILLION VIEWERS? IT'S SOMETHING I NEVER UNDERSTOOD.'
> JOE PASQUALE

LYNNE FRANKS v. JOHN BURTON RACE v. JANICE DICKINSON
series 7

> 'YOU'RE THE MOST HORRIBLE PEOPLE I'VE EVER ENCOUNTERED!'
> LYNNE FRANKS

Lynne Franks, Janice Dickinson and John Burton Race. If you ever want to guarantee carnage, right there are three people who'll serve it up on a plate, and then offer you seconds.

Those three couldn't even agree to disagree.

JANICE DICKINSON: You don't give a f**k?
LYNNE FRANKS: No, I really don't give a f**k!
JANICE DICKINSON: You can do what you want, you shrew.

Incredible. Not since Shakespeare has anyone insulted someone by calling them a shrew. Janice hated Lynne so much that even the sound of Lynne's voice was enough to set her off.

But this experience didn't put Janice off the jungle. She actually returned a couple of years later to appear in the second American series of *I'm A Celebrity … Get Me Out Of Here!*

'I THINK I GOT THE SHORT END OF THE STRAW BECAUSE HOWEVER PRICKLY I CAN BE, AND I'M NO ANGEL, I DO THINK JANICE DICKINSON, RODNEY MARSH AND JOHN BURTON RACE IN ONE SMALL SPACE IS A BIT MUCH FOR ANYBODY'.
LYNNE FRANKS

Almost from the moment that trio arrived in camp back in 2007, Lynne, Janice and John were on each other's backs. And it wasn't just the odd comment – they screamed blue murder at each other around the clock.

Mind you, other than the racket the three of them were making, the jungle had never been more peaceful, because every bird, croc, snake, spider and rat for miles around had run for their lives.

Theirs was some of the worst behaviour I've ever seen, and keep in mind, that's coming from someone whose parents have been known to eat their kids.

In saying all that, John did make a lovely camel-sausage stew, Janice had some great showbiz stories, and Lynne … no, sorry, you'll need to get back to me on that one.

'THE BIGGEST MISTAKE I MADE WAS FORGETTING IT WAS A GAME ON TV. YOU DON'T NOTICE THE CAMERAS AND I STARTED FROM THE BEGINNING REALLY THINKING: OH, THIS IS REAL.'
LYNNE FRANKS

During the first series, I was told that three celebrities were threatening to leave camp. And the only thing that would stop them was if the senior producer on site came and saw them immediately.

I was dispatched to try and resolve things and was met by an angry trio made up of Uri Geller, Tony Blackburn and Darren Day. Their issue revolved around the Bush Telegraph – the place where celebrities are interviewed by producers using an unmanned camera.

It turned out that they'd also been using this room for another purpose entirely – tick checking! Ticks are blood-sucking parasites that are drawn to warm, dark places on your body and then burrow their way into your skin headfirst. They can cause temporary paralysis.

Keeping ticks at bay and avoiding horrible things like paralysis requires regular checking. The celebrities had decided the perfect place to do the checks was the Bush Telegraph.

What they were doing was sticking their hats over the camera lens to give themselves a bit of privacy (the camera is now behind a glass screen, but this was series 1 and we were learning as we went). They'd then proceed to check their most intimate parts using a mirror and various yoga-type positions.

However, one week in, they noticed a second camera in the roof of the hut. They were furious. I promised them that their embarrassment, and ours, had been spared, because the camera in question was faulty. This was the truth – not that they believed me. They threatened all sorts of legal action if it turned out we'd been flashing their privates on the show.

Richard Cowles, Executive Producer and Co-Creator

NATALIE APPLETON v.
SOPHIE ANDERTON
series 4

Two extremely high-maintenance girls. Both of them used to having their way. Neither of them a big fan of sharing the limelight. What could possibly go wrong? Well, as it turned out, everything. Natalie and Sophie managed to conjure arguments out of thin air. Arguments about weird girlie stuff like 'emotions' and 'feelings'. Personally, I didn't have a clue what they were banging on about. But that didn't make it any less scary. I swear, when the two of them went at it, even Janet Street-Porter backed off.

During one of their biggest barneys, Joe Pasquale tried to butt in. It was probably the last time Joe Pasquale will ever butt into anything in his entire life.

'IF IT WAS JUST A COUPLE OF GIRLS HAVING A SPAT, THEN YOU LET IT DIE OUT. BUT THIS WAS ESCALATING, AND I THOUGHT IF I DON'T DO SOMETHING RIGHT NOW, THEN THIS IS GOING TO KICK OFF. THEY BOTH TURNED ON ME LIKE A COUPLE OF BANSHEES.'
JOE PASQUALE

'SHE EXPECTED ME TO BE THE ONE GOING "OOOOOOH!" LIKE THIS AT EVERYTHING. AND I WAS JUST LIKE, OH, GET ON WITH IT. SHE TRIED HER BEST TO TURN THE PUBLIC AGAINST ME AND IT COMPLETELY BACKFIRED ON HER.'
SOPHIE ANDERTON

NATALIE APPLETON: I've had enough of Sophie – me me me me me. Me me me. I'm the best at this. I'm the best at that. Oh I don't care, cos I'm the best at everything. Am I as bad as that? I need to know. I need to know if I'm like this. Because I was sick. Am I a bad person for being f*****g sick?

JANET STREET-PORTER: No.

NATALIE APPLETON: You told me–

SOPHIE ANDERTON: I didn't say it like that at all.

NATALIE APPLETON: You did. You've got no emotions, Sophie. You hugged me.

SOPHIE ANDERTON: I did. I said I was sorry after–

NATALIE APPLETON: You have no emotions. There's no emotions in you.

SOPHIE ANDERTON: I'm not feeling it - cos I won't cry out here.

JOE PASQUALE: Girls. Can we–

NATALIE APPLETON: I'm expressing how I feel! Just give me a sec.

JOE PASQUALE: All right.

NATALIE APPLETON: There's no feelings.

SOPHIE ANDERTON: Yes, there is.

NATALIE APPLETON: No there's not. All you care about is how you look.

SOPHIE ANDERTON: The only reason I climbed up that tree is you didn't want to do it.

NATALIE APPLETON: Because I'm scared of heights and you're NOT!!!

SOPHIE ANDERTON: Well I'm sorry about that, but it's not my fault.

NATALIE APPLETON: No it's not your fault, is it? I wanted to feel you. I don't feel you, babe.

Even now, years later, I look back at this and think … what the hell was she on about?

KIM WOODBURN v. JOE BUGNER
series 9

In the 1970s, Joe Bugner pushed the legendary Muhammad Ali to the wire; he survived a titanic battle with Smokin' Joe Frazier. Frazier only beat him on points. Joe even gave Henry Cooper a beating.

But in all these battles of blood and guts, Bugner never came up against a heavyweight quite like Kim Woodburn.

To the producers, Joe Bugner seemed like the perfect booking. Mainly because he was cheap – he only lived up the road, so they didn't have to buy him a ticket for the plane.

But because Joe was living out in Australia, he seemed to have no idea what the show was about. Now, like anyone who's in discussions about taking part in *I'm A Celebrity … Get Me Out Of Here!*, Joe received the comprehensive information pack, including a DVD of old episodes, and went through long conversations with the casting team.

And like many other celebrities who sign up to go into the jungle, you get the sneaky feeling he didn't watch the DVD and ignored every word the casting team said.

Looking back, Joe seemed to think he was put in camp simply to wind people up. To his credit, he set about doing this with gusto.

Kim took the bait straight away and the two of them were off, rowing and bickering like an old married couple.

There were genuine concerns that the pair of them might come to blows. Someone could have been seriously hurt. After all, Joe hadn't trained for years and Kim looked absolutely lethal.

> **KIM WOODBURN:** If you're not going to cook, hop it and let this man do it.
> **JOE BUGNER:** Sit down.
> **KIM WOODBURN:** Don't you dare speak to me like that!
> **JOE BUGNER:** Sit down.
> **KIM WOODBURN:** Don't you dare speak to me like that. Ever!

As George Hamilton said, Kim is not a woman you want to cross. Looking at Joe's eyes, you could tell he knew he was way out of his depth. If there'd been a referee around, he would've taken an eight count.

DAVID VAN DAY v. EVERYONE
series 8

It's hard to single out who David had a fight with, because he seemed to wind up just about everyone. The only person he had on his side was Joe Swash. Because it is literally impossible to fall out with Joe Swash. I've tried. It can't be done.

Like Joe Bugner, David Van Day was a late arrival.

'THERE IS NO DOUBT ABOUT IT. THE VIEWERS AT HOME LOVE A DEBATE. WELL, A ROW, REALLY. THEY LOVE A GOOD OLD ARGUMENT AND WHEN IT KICKS OFF THEY LAP IT UP.'
DAVID VAN DAY

What is it with these late arrivals? They always convince themselves they need to make a big splash on their entrance. Why would any sensible person think that? You're about to enter a campsite full of exhausted, hungry, grumpy individuals. You're well fed. You're all scrubbed up. Your clothes are ironed and don't smell all smoky and damp. You have absolutely no grasp of the group dynamic or the general mood.

> **'I THINK NICOLA HAD AN INSTANT DISLIKE FOR ME THE MOMENT SHE SAW ME.'**
> DAVID VAN DAY

Common sense would surely suggest playing it low-key. Get in there; get a feel for the place. Suck up to people. Be quiet and humble. Repeat it like a mantra: 'Quiet and humble.'

But not this lot. Oh no – they're celebrities. They have this need to perform. They have to announce themselves with a big 'Ta-dah!'

So David Van Day waltzes in with Timmy Mallett and it all goes downhill from there. Actually, thinking about it, that was David's fatal error.

> **'I THINK ONE OF THE BEST MOMENTS WAS LISTENING TO NICOLA RANT HER LAST RANT AT ME AS SHE LEFT THE JUNGLE.'**
> DAVID VAN DAY

Showing up anywhere in the world with Timmy Mallett as your plus one is not the best way to make a good first impression, is it?

Anyway, David proceeds to fall out with everybody. And just in case there's a celebrity left in camp who's still sitting on the fence, he goes and nicks the comfortable bed on the double-decker bus and gloats about it. (A double-decker bus in a jungle? What the hell was that all about?)

David was your classic pantomime villain. But you have to hand it to him: he made it one of the most watchable series of all.

> **NICOLA McLEAN:** Why don't you crawl into a cave and cry because you're afraid of the dark?
> **DAVID VAN DAY:** I'm not going to cry.

> **'YOUR GAME IS VERY GOOD, BETTER THAN MINE, EVERYONE WATCHING BECAUSE HE'S A SNAKE IN THE GRASS.'**
> NICOLA McLEAN

JOHN LYDON v. KATIE PRICE
series 3

'ALL RIGHT, THIS IS STUPID, THERE'S NO WATER LEFT, THIS IS REALLY F*****G STUPID. HELLO JORDAN, YOU KNOW, WHEN ARE YOU ACTUALLY GOING TO DO SOMETHING? I'M OFF FOR MY WALK. F**K IT.'
JOHN LYDON

It was a miracle they got John Lydon into the jungle in the first place. Nobody expected it, and even when John was on his way, the producers were convinced he'd change his mind and leg it. But into the camp he went. And one of the reasons John decided to give it a go was his love of nature.

I've lived here all my life so I take it for granted, but to people seeing the jungle for the first time, it really is a thing of beauty. It can really take your breath away: the sounds, the smells, feeling the rotting leaves squish under your feet. It's nature at its purest. And John loved it.

Sadly for John, he wasn't in there alone. He was in there with a load of celebrities, and one of them was Katie Price (then Jordan).

Now, Katie Price is many things; but natural she is not.

'SOME PEOPLE DON'T DO NOTHING AT ALL. AND ONE PERSON IN PARTICULAR … YOU KNOW … WHATEVER CAREER THAT THING THINKS SHE HAS IT'S A PRETTY USELESS ONE IN MY BOOKS. LOOK, THERE'S MY CAREER! THEY'RE TWO A PENNY IN ANY CRAP DISCO. IF THAT GIRL LIFTS A FINGER, IT'S ONLY TO DO HER NAILS. SHE'S SO SPOILT, SHE GETS ON MY T**S. I CAN'T STAND HER.'
JOHN LYDON

123

'THE WOMAN'S TALENTLESS. IT DOESN'T DO ANYTHING, AND WHEN IT DOES IT NAGS ALL THE WAY THROUGH IT. IT AIN'T FUNNY ANY MORE. IT DON'T CONTRIBUTE. IT'S A PARASITE. IT OCCUPIES THE CENTRE-OF-ATTENTION BED. BUT IT ISN'T HAPPY EVEN WITH THAT. THE SMOKE ANNOYS HER! IT'S THE CAMPFIRE, B***H! RIGHT. LIVE WITH IT. OR SWAP.'
JOHN LYDON

For someone who's spent his life deliberately causing offence, it was a weird thing to see. Katie Price genuinely offended John, and he didn't know what to do about it. John rarely said anything directly to her. Instead, he would direct all his moans at other celebrities – mainly Lord Brocket – or head to the Bush Telegraph to swear and kick the wall a few times.

What probably wound him up more than anything was that Katie Price really didn't care what he thought of her. She was too busy doing her own thing.

Given that her own thing involved flirting with Peter Andre and lounging around showing off her boob job, John was only ever going to get angrier.

In the end, you'd have to say that Katie Price won the war, because John was the one who walked.

NIGEL BENN v. RHONA CAMERON v. CHRISTINE HAMILTON
series 1

'RHONA, AND I HOPE SHE DOESN'T MIND MY SAYING THIS, CAN BE ONE OF THE MOST ARGUMENTATIVE PEOPLE I'VE EVER KNOWN. AND I THINK SHE'S AWARE OF IT AND SHE LIKES IT. SHE DOES IT ON PURPOSE. THERE WAS A LOT OF FIGHTING GOING ON, PARTICULARLY BETWEEN RHONA AND NIGEL BENN.'
TONY BLACKBURN

Back in 2002, the producers had no idea what was going to happen when they dumped a load of celebrities into a camp in the middle of the Australian rainforest. Would they get along? Would they do anything interesting? Would the whole thing fall flat on its face? It really was a complete gamble. But it wasn't long before that gamble paid off.

Because what we all quickly learnt was that the kind of people who might annoy you a tiny bit if you met them at some posh do in London for five minutes – those people will seriously do your head in if you're stuck in the middle of the jungle with them for two weeks.

And there's absolutely nowhere to go to escape them.

This can only mean one thing … Fights! And lots of them.

And the first ever celebrities to rub each other up the wrong way were comedian Rhona Cameron and boxing champ Nigel Benn.

> 'I THOUGHT, WELL I SHOULD REALLY GET BETWEEN THE TWO OF THEM, BUT I THOUGHT – THAT'S NIGEL BENN.'
> TONY BLACKBURN

NIGEL BENN: If you was a man, I'd knock you sparko.
RHONA CAMERON: I'd love to fight you, Nigel. If I was a boxer, I'd love to.

And it wasn't long before Christine Hamilton, wife of disgraced politician Neil Hamilton, got in on the act.

What happens is, Christine winds up Rhona by telling her that Nigel's religious beliefs mean he thinks she, being gay, is going straight to hell.

The truth is, Nigel never said that.

Anyway, the upshot is that Rhona has a right old go at Nigel. He denies it. And when he finds out who spread the rumour, he's on Christine's case in yet another series 1 bust-up.

CHRISTINE HAMILTON: Okay, if that's what you think, there's no point in discussing it further.
NIGEL BENN: It is. There's no point discussing it. Just stay away from me.
CHRISTINE HAMILTON: All right, I will.
NIGEL BENN: It's just gone from one to another. Because you've gone and–
CHRISTINE HAMILTON: I'm not prepared to–
NIGEL BENN: No, no, no. No, go away from me you stupid old woman.

12

WINNERS AND LOSERS

'I REALLY DID ENJOY IT. I COULD HAVE STAYED IN THERE LIKE SOME OLD VIETNAM GEEZER HIDING OUT IN THE BUSH FOR ANOTHER YEAR – YOU'D FIND ME THERE WITH LEMBIT [ÖPIK] ON THE NEXT SERIES.'
SHAUN RYDER

YOU MIGHT THINK I'm just a cockroach who enjoys scaring the pants off a load of celebrities.

And you'd be right.

But every now and then, someone passes through the jungle that even I have a soft spot for. Invariably it's someone who gives it their all, who makes us laugh and cry and, most importantly, actually seems to enjoy their time in the rainforest.

They come on the show for all the right reasons and they have an absolute ball. They aren't always the easiest people to live with. They aren't always the most stable of individuals. But when they leave, the jungle's always a lesser place without them.

This lot might not have won the actual crown, but these are my jungle heroes.

THE WINNERS
DAVID GEST, series 6

'I WAS 100 PER CENT DAVID GEST'S BITCH WHEN I WAS IN THE JUNGLE. LOOKING BACK NOW, I WAS VERY MUCH USED. HE USED ME.'
MATT WILLIS

Nobody knew who David Gest was when he arrived in the jungle. Sure, we knew he was pals with Michael Jackson. We'd read in magazines that he'd got married to Liza Minnelli. And we'd seen pictures. In which, let's face it, the guy looked pretty weird. He had this thing going on with his hair, like he had a load of spray-painted Brillo Pads glued to his head.

But within days of arriving he'd revealed a sparky, quirky, bonkers personality that was hard to resist. David was without a doubt the jungle's greatest ever storyteller. But don't take my word for it. Here he is in full flow, winding up Myleene Klass.

MYLEENE KLASS: What's your background, where are you from?

DAVID GEST: I was born in Taiwan. My father was a fisherman. My mother was a nun. And then they gave me up. She had the baby illegally. And they left me in China with this family. It's really sad, because I had no parents for the first three years. I was in an orphanage and then I was adopted by this family that came from America.

MYLEENE KLASS: Were you? Serious? Really?

DAVID GEST: Yeah. My father had one leg and my mother had one leg.

David's other legendary creations were the charity Chinese Girls With Herpes (a viewer even created a website for them) and his maid, Vaginika Semen. I think you spell that with a 'K', but really, who the hell knows?

A class act.

GEORGE HAMILTON, series 9

'GEORGE, BE GENTLE WITH ME, WON'T YOU?'
KIM WOODBURN

George Hamilton was my favourite ever celebrity. Me and [Casting Executive] Daisy Moore had been chasing him for years. We met him in London to try to get him to do a previous series and it never worked out. We always met at these posh hotels – it was Claridge's in London that time – he was so glamorous. Lunch always went on for hours and he'd tell you all these stories about the stars he'd hung out with. He was funny and charming and I was desperate to get him into the jungle.

Anyway, we went to meet him in Beverly Hills a couple of years later, and this time he said yes. He had a new girlfriend. She was the surgeon who'd just performed his knee surgery. Now he was going out with her. She was about thirty-five!

She thought it would be good for him – a bit of fresh air and exercise. And he was an absolute dream booking. He was even better than I'd hoped and he loved it in there.

Natalka Znak, Executive Producer and Co-Creator

George Hamilton. A Hollywood legend. A jungle giant. But above all, a gentleman.

George was one of the older campers to join the show, but he took everything in his stride. His relationship with Kim Woodburn gave us some classic moments, but what he gave us most of all was his wisdom:

'IT'S A STRANGE THING I'VE NOTICED, BUT WITH WOMEN, THEY WANT HONESTY, AND YET SOMETIMES THEY GET UPSET IF YOU'RE HONEST. SO YOU HAVE TO KNOW WHEN TO BE HONEST, AND THEY HAVE THESE LITTLE REALITY CHECKS TO SEE IF YOU'RE REALLY LOOKING AND WATCHING. FOR INSTANCE, YOU'RE GOING OUT TO DINNER AND MY GIRLFRIEND WILL SAY TO ME, "HOW DO YOU THINK I LOOK?"

AND IF I SAY, "GREAT," AND I'M LOOKING DOWN, YOU CAN'T DO THAT. SO I LOOK VERY CLOSELY AT EVERYTHING AND I SAY, "I LIKE IT, BUT THE SHOES - YOU GOTTA CHANGE THE SHOES."

AND SHE SAYS, "DO YOU THINK SO?"

NOW, WHAT SHE LOVES IS THE IDEA THAT SHE CAN NOW GO AND TRY SOME OTHER PAIRS OF SHOES ON … FINALLY SHE SAYS TO ME, "I APPRECIATE SO MUCH THAT YOU LOOK AT THESE DETAILS."

OR SHE'LL SAY TO ME SOMETIMES, "DO YOU THINK I'M GAINING ANY WEIGHT?"

AND I SAY, "WELL, YOU'RE GAINING IT, BUT YOU'RE GAINING IT IN THE RIGHT PLACES."

THEN SHE'LL SAY, "NO, I CAN SEE I'M GETTING FAT RIGHT HERE," AND I SAY, "WELL THEN, RUN A LITTLE."

"YOU'RE RIGHT, I NEED TO RUN." NEXT THING IS SHE'S RUNNING EVERYWHERE … SO IMMEDIATELY IF I'M HONEST AND PAY ATTENTION TO HER AND GIVE HER ADVICE, THEY LOVE IT.

MOST GUYS JUST SAY, "YEAH, YOU LOOK GREAT." BIG MISTAKE. THEY DON'T TRUST YOU AFTER THAT.'
GEORGE HAMILTON

Brilliant advice, which I put to use immediately on one of my wives. And just like George said, she went running.

Straight out the door. Never saw her again.

But I still love the guy. I hear George namedrops about me these days, when he's telling stories to Brad Pitt and the rest of the Hollywood crowd.

JOHN LYDON, series 3

John Lydon. What a guy.

I remember one day, as he lay in his hammock, gazing reflectively up through the jungle canopy, I said to him, 'John, has the jungle changed you?'

'**** off, you little ****, before I **** you in the **** and **** you, right in your ******* face, you ******* ****!'

Ah, John. I'll always remember those words fondly. A sweet, sweet man.

> 'I'M SITTING IN A LEAKY F*****G SOAKING BUNK. YOU'RE TAKING THE P**S. IT'S A JOKE. RIGHT.. I'M GOING IN THE MORNING'
> JOHN LYDON

Nobody ever thought he'd do it. But John Lydon was my dream booking and I thought it'd be worth giving it a go, so I managed to persuade his agent to set up a meeting and I flew out to America to speak to him.

I had arrived late the previous night and by our lunchtime meeting I had a serious dose of jetlag, so when I went to meet John I was not at my best.

Despite being at a swanky Hollywood hotel and having lunch in a beautiful palm-tree garden, the meeting was awful. He was really rude. He kept on insisting he didn't want to do it.

And I had this jetlag headache pounding away. So I ended up saying, 'Fine. Either do it or don't. It's your decision, John. I really don't care.' (Not exactly the type of Hollywood schmoozing that usually goes on in that town!)

I went home and apparently John had phoned his manager and said, 'I just had a really weird meeting with that woman. She didn't even want me to do the show.'

So being John Lydon, the moment he thought we didn't want him, he was up for it. There was also the fact that John really loves nature. I'd said to him how rough it was in there. We always make it clear to celebrities just how tough it really is. We gave what Richard [Cowles, Executive Producer] and I call 'The Talk of Doom'. As in, we honestly tell every potential participant how gruelling it really is, so when it gets tough they can't say, 'I would never have done it if I'd known.'

With some celebrities, that's the reason they back off. But with John it was a big selling point.

Still, even after he signed up, we still never actually believed he'd do it. Our attitude was, 'Let's just get him on the plane.' Then, when he did that, we thought, 'Let's just get him to the hotel.' Then when he did that, it was, 'Let's just try and get him into the camp.'

Once he was in there, we took each day as it came. John threatened to leave constantly. We kind of got used to it. He really, really hated Jordan. Mainly because he knew she'd be getting loads of attention back home.

When John finally did walk out, I was rushing over to meet him – it was near the Trials Clearing. Just as I caught sight of him I fell over – properly toppled down a slope head over heels.

He was actually lovely to me then. In the car back to the hotel, he even gave me his hat. Signed it and handed it over. I made a mate for life.

Natalka Znak, Executive Producer and Co-Creator

I genuinely admire all the celebrities that appeared on the first series, because they were pioneers; they had literally no idea what they were getting themselves into. They didn't have tapes of previous series to watch. They simply heard us pitching them the idea and were brave enough to say yes.

True courage indeed.

But I suppose, wearing my producer's hat, my favourite single celebrity has to be John Lydon. Not because he was particularly nice to me – in fact, he called me a number of rude names while he was in the jungle – but because he represented a major casting coup. His status as a popular-culture icon and master of rebellion made his appearance on the show all the more unexpected, and although he ultimately walked out in another act of rebellion, his appearance on the show opened the way for other high-profile celebrities to take part in subsequent series. The fact that John had done it set a precedent.

Richard Cowles, Executive Producer and Co-Creator

'IF I HAD TO SUM UP MY TIME IN THE JUNGLE, I'D LIKE TO SAY IT'S BEEN ONE HELL OF AN EXPERIENCE.'
DAVID VAN DAY

DAVID VAN DAY, series 8

We'd just worked with David Van Day on a show called *Pop Goes the Band*. We reformed Dollar for it and David got a facelift.

He was hilarious – he was one of those people who were always on the list for *I'm A Celebrity*, but on paper don't look like a good booking.

But I got on well with him, and he was just absolutely brilliant on the show.

Natalka Znak, Executive Producer and Co-Creator

For the producers, David was the ultimate baddie – he just loved stirring things up. And they know you lot just lap that up.

From the moment he arrived in camp side by side with Timmy Mallett, to the day he was voted off, David caused the kind of irritation a whole squadron of mosquitoes could only dream of.

He wound up the camp, and when they gave him a hard time he got his revenge by sleeping in a lovely dry double-decker bus, while they lay soaking in a torrential downpour.

Love him or hate him, you can't deny David Van Day is a genuine one-off.

David's such a character. When I went to his house for his clothes fitting, he tried all the different outfits on. He was actually in pretty good shape because he'd gone on a diet to get ready for the jungle. But then he didn't get dressed afterwards. He was just running around in his pants.

In the end, I had to tell him to go and put some trousers on.

Daisy Moore, Casting Executive

SHAUN RYDER,
series 10

'I DO APOLOGIZE FOR THE LANGUAGE – I'M VERY SORRY.'
SHAUN RYDER

Shaun was lovely. When we met him for the show, he wasn't bothered about doing any of the Trials. None of that stuff fazed him at all. The only thing he was worried about was that the other people in the camp would drive him round the bend.

And as it turned out, we put him in there with Gillian McKeith.

Daisy Moore, Casting Executive

133

For many viewers, Shaun Ryder is the all-time greatest celebrity ever to set foot in the jungle. He had all the madness, anarchy and unpredictability of John Lydon, but unlike John, Shaun saw it right through to the end.

The only person who wasn't a fan was *I'm A Celebrity … Get Me Out Of Here!*'s bleep man. He sprained a wrist trying to keep up with Shaun's potty mouth.

There were classic moments. Who will ever forget Shaun's run-in with a bad-tempered snake in the overnight challenge? Ninety-nine per cent of celebrities would have been screaming for their agent, for an ambulance, for someone to get them the hell out of there. Not Shaun Ryder. Not his style.

'OH, YOU DIRTY B*****D. I WILL PULL YOU OUT AND I WILL ******* ****.'
SHAUN RYDER TO THE SNAKE

What a hero. And Shaun didn't have any time for Gillian McKeith's nonsense either, which only made us love him all the more.

'I FEEL TERRIBLE ABOUT THE SWEARING, BUT I JUST CAN'T HELP IT. IT SAVES THROWING HER OFF A BRIDGE.'
SHAUN RYDER ON GILLIAN McKEITH

In the end, Shaun came second to Stacey Solomon, and he was more than happy with that.

A Madchester legend. A genuine jungle star.

JOEY ESSEX, series 13

'I'M NOT A VERY CONFRONTATIONAL PERSON. I'LL ONLY EVER CONFRONTATE SOMEONE IF IT'S FOR A PURPOSE…'
JOEY ESSEX

I don't think I've ever come across anyone quite like Joey Essex.

When Joey was booked on the show, people across Britain expected him to be a shallow, slightly dim geezer with a fake tan and ridiculously white teeth. The kind of person many of us normally wouldn't give the time of day to. Turns out if you did give Joey the time of day, he wouldn't have a clue what you were talking about. On their first night in the jungle, Amy Willerton had to teach Joey how to use a clock.

But for all the gaps in his education, Joey turned out to be a genuinely lovely bloke. Plus he's good at counting and emptying the Dunny, which makes him prime marriage material in my book.

'WHAT DOES IMMUNITY MEAN?'
JOEY ESSEX

THE LOSERS

For every winner, there has to be a loser.

These are the celebrities who drive you round the bend. Their behaviour infuriates you. Their voice gets right up your nose. You spend night after night shouting at the telly. You tell your mates how much you hate them.

And it's only after they walk out or get the boot that you realize what good value they were.

Funny that, isn't it?

MATTHEW WRIGHT, series 13

ALFONSO RIBEIRO: Okay, Matthew, enough!

MATTHEW WRIGHT: You just said it.

ALFONSO RIBEIRO: Enough!

MATTHEW WRIGHT: Okay.

ALFONSO RIBEIRO: Okay. Enough! I have had enough of your f*****g s**t!

Matthew Wright. What a guy. I know ticks that cause less irritation.

Why is Matthew on my roll call of rogues? Well, for one thing, he blubbed after taking on his first Bushtucker Trial.

And for another, he's Matthew Wright.

And if you think I'm being a bit harsh, I've got just two words for you: WHITE. BIKINI.

The prosecution rests.

SCOTT HENSHALL, series 6

Before he arrived in the jungle, I heard that Scott Henshall was the fashion designer everyone was wearing.

And sure enough, I found him very wearing indeed.

Scott was chosen to do aload of Trials, but he'd barely dip a toe in before he'd shout, 'I'm a celebrity – get me out of here!'

> 'I DON'T WANT TO EAT ANYTHING UNTIL I GET TO McDONALD'S. NOTHING.'
> SCOTT HENSHALL

It drove Ant and Dec crazy. As with Helen Flanagan, there would be an endless amount of waiting around while Scott debated whether or not he'd be taking on the latest Trial.

And all this time the camera guys, the sound guys, the producers and our hosts would be thinking the same thing: 'It's flippin' lunchtime, mate! Would you please get a move on!'

Apparently Scott brought out a new line of underwear after he got home. Scaredy pants!

FREDDIE STARR, series 11

'FREDDIE STARR PROMISED EVERYTHING. VERY FUNNY, A BIT OF A WRECK. AND I SAY THAT IN THE NICEST POSSIBLE WAY.'
JANET STREET-PORTER

Just how crazy is Freddie Starr?

Well, here's a good example that never made the show. After he's won the Greasy Spoon Eating Trial against Mark Wright, Freddie asks Ant and Dec what the tie-break challenge would have been.

The boys put a revolting smoothie on the table so Mark and Freddie can see what they'd have been faced with.

Without blinking an eye, Freddie downs his smoothie in one go.

At that moment, you saw what might have been if Freddie could only have lasted the course. Sadly, an allergic reaction put paid to Freddie's challenge and he was on his way to A&E before anybody knew what was happening. Such a shame.

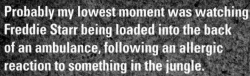

Probably my lowest moment was watching Freddie Starr being loaded into the back of an ambulance, following an allergic reaction to something in the jungle.

Freddie had been one of my childhood heroes and one of the few celebrities I was genuinely in awe of meeting.

To see him in a bad way, not knowing how it was going to turn out, was pretty tough.

Richard Cowles, Executive Producer and Co-Creator

DAVID VAN DAY, series 8

'"BIFF BAFF BOFF" WAS HORRENDOUS. BUT THEY ACTUALLY THOUGHT IT WAS GOING TO BE CHRISTMAS NUMBER ONE. BRILLIANT. THEY'RE DELUDED.'
NICOLA McLEAN

'I CAN'T UNDERSTAND WHY THEY DIDN'T BRING IT OUT AS A SINGLE. I WOULD HAVE IMMEDIATELY PLAYED IT BECAUSE IT WAS SO FUNNY.'
TONY BLACKBURN

 Yes. I know he was in my winners list. But by any definition David Van Day is a loser too.

I mean, have you heard 'Biff Baff Boff – We're Celebrities'?

'WE HAD HIGH HOPES. AND DO YOU KNOW WHAT? I THINK EVERYBODY ELSE DID AS WELL. THEY THOUGHT THEY WERE GOING TO COME OUT THAT JUNGLE AND "BIFF BAFF BOFF" MIGHT BE NUMBER ONE. THEY'D NEVER LIVE IT DOWN.'
DAVID VAN DAY

HELEN FLANAGAN, series 12

Helen Flanagan – or 'hit the redial', as she appeared to be known back in the UK – was the ultimate 'can't do' girl. Thanks to Helen's performances at the Bushtucker Trials, I missed three rounds of golf with Ant and Dec, a manicure, two hair appointments (I know I don't have any hair – they just buff me up) and a chanting session with my guru. And fellow celebrity Colin Baker lost several kilos.

I didn't strike Helen off my Christmas-card list. I'm not petty. But I did put something special in the envelope.

My main memory of Helen Flanagan is that her biggest concern the day before going into the jungle was making sure we gave her time for another spray tan.

David Harvey, Casting Executive

GILLIAN McKEITH, series 10

ANT: Gillian, you claim to have phobias of spiders, insects, bugs, water, rats, crocodiles ... and heights. What on earth made you come onto this show?
GILLIAN McKEITH: I must have lost my marbles.

Gillian was hard work for everyone at the Trials. She drove Ant and Dec nuts, she had Medic Bob running around like a blue-arsed fly, and she had the celebrities back in camp munching away on a diet of rice, beans and despair.

I would tell Gillian to stick to the day job. But considering her day job is rummaging about in people's poo, maybe not.

Gillian McKeith was my favourite contestant. Great content. She provided loads of stories, she had a larder in her knickers, she wound everybody up. She should never have been in the jungle – she was terrified of everything. She was a dream.

Becca Walker, Executive Producer

THE FIRST OUT

'YOU'VE PUT YOURSELF THROUGH GOING INTO CAMP. YOU'VE PUT UP WITH EVERYBODY ELSE. AND TO BE THE FIRST PERSON VOTED OUT IS HUMILIATING.'

JANET STREET-PORTER

As we all know, not everybody can be crowned King or Queen of the Jungle.

Not everybody even comes close.

And every year one unfortunate celebrity suffers the humiliation of being the first person voted out of the camp. Not the first to leave – some people hotfoot it long before the vote-offs start – but the first person the public can't be bothered picking up the phone for.

These are the celebrities who got the boot first in series 1–13:

- URI GELLER
- SIAN LLOYD
- MIKE READ
- NANCY SORRELL
- TOMMY CANNON

- TOBY ANSTIS
- MARC BANNERMAN
- ROBERT KILROY-SILK
- LUCY BENJAMIN
- SHERYL GASCOIGNE

- STEFANIE POWERS
- NADINE DORRIES
- ANNABEL GILES

Now, if there's one thing we know about celebrities, it's that they need to be loved. So being the first person voted out of camp is just about the worst thing that could possibly happen to them. Don't be fooled by the way they punch the air, grab their bag and bound over that bridge. Trust me, when they hear their name called out, a little bit of them dies.

Of course, being the mature, well-adjusted grown-ups they are, there's only one way to respond.

They start blaming everyone else.

What do I mean? Well, for example, when Uri Geller becomes the first celebrity to be voted out in series 1, he decides the public must have been confused about the voting system and got things the wrong way round. He reckons they thought they were voting for their least favourite celebrity.

So as far as Uri's concerned, getting the fewest votes made him, by definition, the most popular guy in there.

Now that is positive thinking.

The other approach, adopted by many 'early leavers', is to blame the way the show was edited. 'Yes, I was the funniest, wackiest, most adorable celebrity in there, but those silly producers – they just missed it.'

So: getting voted out first hurts. But on the plus side, you do get to spend the next ten days lounging around the ridiculously luxurious Versace hotel. And if you get really lucky, I might even invite you to my private suite for drinks.

It hasn't happened yet. I'm just saying it could.

> 'YOU ARE SITTING THERE ABSOLUTELY PRAYING, THINKING I DON'T WANT TO BE THE FIRST ONE OUT, BECAUSE I DON'T CARE WHAT PEOPLE SAY, THAT'S GOT TO HURT A LITTLE BIT. YOU WERE THE MOST UNPOPULAR PERSON IN THE JUNGLE – WHICH SUCKS.'
> MATT WILLIS

THE JUNGLE WALKOUTS

There have been plenty of walkouts over the years. Here's just a few of the celebrities who hit the road before you got a chance to send them packing.

DANNIELLA WESTBROOK,
series 2 (9 days)

> 'I MISS MY KIDS. I MISS KEVIN. AND I MISS CHOCOLATE.'
> DANNIELLA WESTBROOK

JOHN LYDON,
series 3 (11 days)

> 'BYE-BYE.'
> JOHN LYDON

BRIAN HARVEY,
series 4 (6 days)

NATALIE APPLETON,
series 4 (9 days)

'I'M OUT OF HERE. I NEED A BIG MAC, LARGE FRIES, A BATH, A SHAVE, CHANGE OF CLOTHES, BLEACH ME HAIR AND MAYBE A SPRAY TAN. THAT'S WHAT I NEED.'
BRIAN HARVEY

'I FEEL LIKE I'VE BEEN WRINGED OUT ... AND THE WATER'S GONE.'
NATALIE APPLETON

'SHE JUST COULDN'T TAKE IT ANY MORE, SO NOBODY WAS SURPRISED WHEN SHE SAID SHE WAS LEAVING.'
JANET STREET-PORTER

'AT THE TIME IT GOT SO BAD AND SO HEATED THAT IT LED TO BRIAN WALKING OUT.'
JOE PASQUALE

CAMILLA DALLERUP,
series 9 (4 days)

JUSTIN RYAN: Do you want me to get you some choccies?
CAMILLA DALLERUP: No.

KATIE PRICE,
series 9 (9 days)

'I'VE HAD SO MUCH S**T, I JUST DON'T
WANT TO BE HERE ANY MORE.'
KATIE PRICE

Fair enough. Bye!

GEORGE HAMILTON,
series 9 (15 days)

FREDDIE STARR,
series 11 (1 day)

'AT THIS POINT IN MY LIFE, I HAVE
TO WEIGH WHAT IS IMPORTANT
TO ME AS FAR AS MY LIFE GOES
AS OPPOSED TO THIS.'
GEORGE HAMILTON

'WHEN HE LEFT I WAS SAD. IT WAS
NEVER QUITE THE SAME FOR ME.
I'M GOING TO MISS YOU.'
KIM WOODBURN

'I GREW UP WATCHING HIM –
HE ALWAYS USED TO MAKE ME LAUGH.'
FATIMA WHITBREAD

MALCOLM McLAREN,
series 7 (0 days)

Malcolm McLaren. Now there was a character.

Actually, that's only a guess. I never met the man. The nearest Malcolm ever got to the jungle was the side salad he ordered from room service when he arrived at the hotel.

Because the day the celebrities were due to head into camp, Malcolm changed his mind. And there was no talking him round. In the end, they just flew him home. Crazy.

Mind you, he flew first class all the way, so maybe he wasn't so daft after all.

To be fair to him, it wasn't really Malcolm. It was his girlfriend, Young Kim. She was worried about Malcom doing the show. She'd obviously heard something about it and she asked him not to go in.

The thing is, Bob had done the usual medical talk to everyone, and that talk always put the fear of God into people.

And Richard and I had also given Malcolm our Talk of Doom.

So anyway, Bob spoke to Young on the phone. He spoke to Malcolm again, too, but nothing worked.

To be honest, we thought it'd be like John [Lydon] again. You know, we'd battle to get him to the hotel, then we'd battle to get him into camp, then we'd battle every day to stop him walking. But this time it just never happened.

Normally between me, Daisy [Moore, Casting Executive] and Medic Bob, we can talk them round.

It's a shame. He'd have hated every minute, but still …

Natalka Znak, Executive Producer and Co-Creator

I took Malcolm for dinner each night in Australia. And he was fine – he was a brilliant raconteur and he was very indiscreet – they were great dinners. And each night he said he was going to do it.

But when he got back to the hotel, he was calling home and being told not to do it. So over the course of the night his mind would change, and then I'd have to persuade him all over again.

On the day they were meant to go in, Natalka and me went to his room and the door was locked. But he'd given me a key so we let ourselves in. He was there. He told us he wasn't doing it. He flew back to the UK that night.

Daisy Moore, Casting Executive

BOARDING PASS
PASSENGER TICKET AND BAGGAGE CHECK

GATE 7

GATE C

Class
First Class

Departure
New York

R No
023 07654 009

For me, there's a whole category of celebrities who just blew it, who never really showed up. It's a group who seem to think that just their name will be enough to win them a load of votes. And when they get evicted, they can't believe it.

But you can't fool the public. They're way too smart for that. If you aren't prepared to engage with the experience, they'll see right through you.

For me Vic Reeves was one. He was a late arrival, and when he did go in, he did very little. I think he really believed his fans would keep him in there till the end.

After he got kicked out, Vic had a word with me. He said he'd been badly edited. It was my fault! But I said to him, 'Vic, all you did in there was whittle bits of wood!' It's true – he just sat there making things out of sticks. I mean, how's that good telly?

Mike Read was another. He was the first out and said we'd edited him really badly. But as far as I could see Mike spent hours in there just writing a diary about the experience – jotting down stuff that was going on and doing little cartoons. We're never going to show someone writing. It's just not going to happen.

Razor Ruddock we thought would be great – he was brilliant when we met him in London. But my guess is he didn't like being hungry and he basically just sat about looking unhappy for a couple of weeks.

Robert Kilroy-Silk was another. We worked for years to get him. He turned us down again and again, then finally he said he'd do it. We were over the moon. We thought he'd be dynamite. Then he goes in and just sort of sits around, staring at the fire for days on end.

It's so frustrating. They promise so much and then don't do anything. And when they get voted out early they often blame the editing.

Natalka Znak, Executive Producer and Co-Creator

13

HUNKS AND BABES

'YOU'VE GOT TO HAVE
A HUNK IN THERE. AND
YOU'VE GOT TO HAVE A
BABE IN THERE – A BIT
OF EYE CANDY.'
KERRY KATONA

NO JUNGLE is complete without a bit of window dressing. And I'm not talking about that daft double-decker bus they had one year. So along with the TV legends, the sports stars and the controversial figures, the producers always make sure to book a few celebrities who are, let's just say, easy on the eye. It's a gamble, because you never quite know what these guys will bring to the jungle, other than a suitcase full of saucy underwear.

Sometimes they turn out to be great characters like Nicola McLean – all feisty and outspoken. Other times they turn out to be Nell McAndrew.

Poor old Nell. One week into that first series, I thought her microphone was broken.

Over the years, that camp has seen some very impressive cleavages: Katie Price's, Ashley Roberts' … Eric Bristow's. Yes, if you've got a hot bod, there's nothing like wandering around the jungle in a bikini to boost your popularity and win some votes.

The younger celebrities are well aware of this. And more often than not, it's when the evictions are on that the clothes come off. The moment those phone lines open, you'll find our sexy young things diving into the pool or heading off to the shower for the third time that day.

But things don't always go to plan with these bookings. In 2011, Aussie lingerie model Emily Scott was hired to be that year's gorgeous blonde. So when she showed up at the hotel with her hair dyed bright pink, there was a bit of a panic. A runner was immediately dispatched to the chemist to pick up a pack of bleach. The result was a sort of washed-out pinkish-grey.

Mind you, she still looked absolutely gorgeous.

'IF YOU'RE A CHICK, YOU'RE GOING TO WASH IN A BIKINI, BUT IF YOU HAPPEN TO BE REALLY HOT AND IN A NICE BIKINI, SO BE IT.'
MATT WILLIS

BRUCEY'S TOP TEN SEXIEST GIRLS

Interestingly, there were way more gorgeous girls to choose from for this list than for the list of handsome fellas. Which, if nothing else, suggests that the casting for *I'm A Celebrity … Get Me Out Of Here!* is done mainly by blokes.

But anyway, here's my top ten of the jungle's sexiest girls. Let me tell you, the competition was very tough. I spent hours poring over pictures of the candidates for the top ten. And I do mean hours.

Okay, days.

As you'll see, some incredibly beautiful women didn't even make it onto the list. And if any of those women would like to take me out to dinner to try to talk me round, I'd be more than happy to hear from them.

1 EMILY SCOTT

4 KATIE PRICE

2 MYLEENE KLASS

3 ASHLEY ROBERTS

7 KAYLA COLLINS

5 CARLY ZUCKER

6 NICOLA McLEAN

8 AMY WILLERTON

9 CATALINA GUIRADO

10 GEMMA ATKINSON

BRUCEY'S TOP TEN SEXIEST BOYS

I was told we needed a list of the top ten sexiest men for the book. It's really not my area of expertise, so I asked the ladies on the production team to come up with one. Due to a careless oversight on their part, I've made a tiny amendment to the list.

1 MARK WRIGHT

Brucey

2 DOUGIE POYNTER

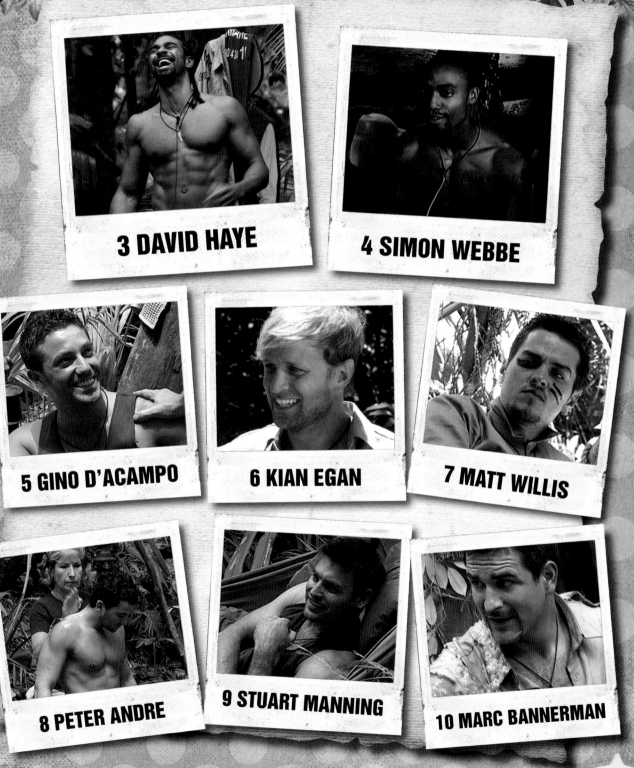

3 DAVID HAYE

4 SIMON WEBBE

5 GINO D'ACAMPO

6 KIAN EGAN

7 MATT WILLIS

8 PETER ANDRE

9 STUART MANNING

10 MARC BANNERMAN

SNAKE
ROCK

14

HOW TO SURVIVE THE JUNGLE

TOP TIPS FROM THE CELEBRITIES

'IF THERE WAS ONE THING I'D DO DIFFERENTLY IF I WENT BACK, IT'S JUST TO KEEP MY MOUTH SHUT MORE. GO OFF INTO THE CORNER, DO A BIT MORE MEDITATION.'

LYNNE FRANKS

SURVIVING IN THE JUNGLE isn't easy for your average star. After all, it's a daunting prospect for a celebrity to have to go three weeks without all the things they care about most: their clothes, their shoes, their make-up, their hair stylist, their mobile phone, their agent, their nail file, their favourite biscuits …

… oh, yeah. And their family.

But the experience genuinely does change them. During those first few terrifying nights, the tiniest noise will have the whole camp jumping out of their skins. But by the end of week three, they're all strutting around like they own the place.

So what valuable words of advice do our star campers – the ones who've been there and done it – have for anyone out there who might be considering a trip to the depths of the jungle?

None.

Look, they're a load of celebrities, so it's a bunch of wishy-washy blah-di-blah about being true to yourself, reaching out to your fellow man and being at one with nature.

Fat lot of use that'll do you when you're staring at the business end of a brown snake.

Anyway, here are all their top tips. If you are visiting the jungle, print these wise words off onto a sheet of A4 paper. And when you get there, use that paper to light your first campfire.

'MY PERSONAL SECRET TO SURVIVING THE JUNGLE? ACCEPTING PEOPLE, LISTENING A LOT AND RUNNING THAT MENTAL MARATHON – JUST DEALING WITH IT, BABES.'
CHARLIE BROOKS

Katie Price purchased a large bottle of Chanel No. 5 at the airport, and prior to going into the jungle sprayed the entire contents all over her jungle gear to combat the smell of smoke from the fire and general dirtiness. She's the only celebrity ever to make a competitive return on the UK show – and she'd clearly learned her lesson from 2004.

David Harvey, Casting Executive

'YOU KNOW WHAT I TOOK FROM THE WHOLE EXPERIENCE WAS, I LEARNT TOLERANCE, I LEARNT TO KEEP MY MOUTH SHUT ... OCCASIONALLY.'
JANET STREET-PORTER

'IT IS INCREDIBLY TOUGH IN THERE. BUT THE ONE SAVING GRACE IS THE PEOPLE YOU HAVE IN THERE WITH YOU. FOR ME ESPECIALLY IT WAS THE JASONS AND THE DAVIDS. AND THEY REALLY DO GET YOU THROUGH IT IN A NON-CHEESY WAY. PLUS AS LONG AS YOU'VE GOT SOMEONE ENTERTAINING YOU'RE ALL RIGHT. GOING IN THERE, WHO WOULD HAVE THOUGHT THAT I WOULD STILL BE INCREDIBLY GOOD FRIENDS WITH DAVID GEST? YOU KNOW, YOU WOULD NEVER PUT US TOGETHER.'
MATT WILLIS

'THE BIGGEST SECRET TO SURVIVING THE JUNGLE IS TO NOT TRY PLAYING ANY GAME. YOU JUST BE YOU.'
PETER ANDRE

THE DUNNY

'I DON'T FEEL
I CAN COUNSEL YOU
WHEN I'M HAVING A S**T.'
STEVE DAVIS TO ANNABEL GILES

PICTURE THE SCENE: you're at a music festival. It's late in the evening on day three and you need the toilet.

You curse inwardly, because you know that no amount of alcohol can prepare you for the next five minutes of your life.

The Portaloo is dark; it's filthy; the stench makes your eyes water like you've been maced. There's no hot water, no toilet paper, and no proper flush because the pump button gave up on day two. Just sitting down takes every ounce of courage you can muster because there's some sort of stuff all round the seat.

Compared to the Dunny, readers, that is pure, unbridled, five-star luxury.

Seriously. After three weeks of the Dunny, your average celebrity would hop into that Portaloo and sniff the air like it was a breeze in a spring meadow.

You'd struggle to get them out.

The point I'm making is that the Dunny is nasty. Not 'I don't really want to do that' nasty. The Dunny is 'No matter how long I live, even if I make it to ninety, this will be the last thing I think of before I die' nasty.

If I go anywhere near the Dunny, I hold my breath. And I'm a cockroach – I can survive a nuclear war. So exactly what is the Dunny?

Well, it's a perfectly innocent wooden structure with a curtain, a seat with a hole in it, and a bucket underneath. Before the celebrities arrive it is odourless.

Then they check into camp. And twenty-four hours later they've turned it into the devil's dung pile.

It doesn't take a rocket scientist to work out why.

'INNIT GOOD? I'M HAVING A DUMP AND I'VE GOT AN AUDIENCE.' LAILA MORSE

The night before the celebrities head into the jungle, they're so worried about the starvation to come that they shovel enough grub down their gobs to last a month. They're told not to, but nobody listens.

Then, fully loaded, they head into camp. Next morning, what with them being all unsettled and scared after their first night of alfresco sleeping, things get a little messy. I'll leave the rest to your imagination.

Then they spend the next three weeks on a diet of rice, beans and animals' naughty bits.

As a result, one of the least popular jobs in camp is the changing of the Dunny barrel, which is a bit like the changing of the guard, but with a lot less ceremony – and you wouldn't want the Queen to see it.

In brief, every few days, two celebrities have to reach below the Dunny and pull out a barrel of poo and wee. They take this barrel to a meeting point, where two crew members swap the full barrel for an empty one.

The two celebrities then return to camp. The two crew members head off to find a mirror, which they look in while asking themselves how their lives went so badly wrong.

Anyway, if you're a celebrity and you're reading this hoping to get some advice about how to cope with the horrors of the jungle … I'm all out.

When it comes to the Dunny, you're on your own.

Nobody wants to deal with the Dunny – for obvious reasons. A while back, there was a debate between the Art Department and unit (the team who manage the site) over who would be responsible for disposing of the Dunny waste.

If the Dunny waste was declared an 'on-screen' item, the problem would belong to the Art Department. If it was an 'off-screen' item, it would be unit's job. Sadly for unit, it was decided that the barrel of poo was an off-screen item and it was down to them.

Helen Kruger-Bratt, Production Executive

'I'VE NEVER HAD EXPERIENCE OF CAMPING OR LIVING OUTDOORS IN THE PAST. OH, I DID ONCE … I STAYED IN A TENT IN MY FRIEND'S GARDEN. ONLY FOR A FEW HOURS THOUGH. WE DIDN'T LIKE IT.' JESSICA-JANE CLEMENT

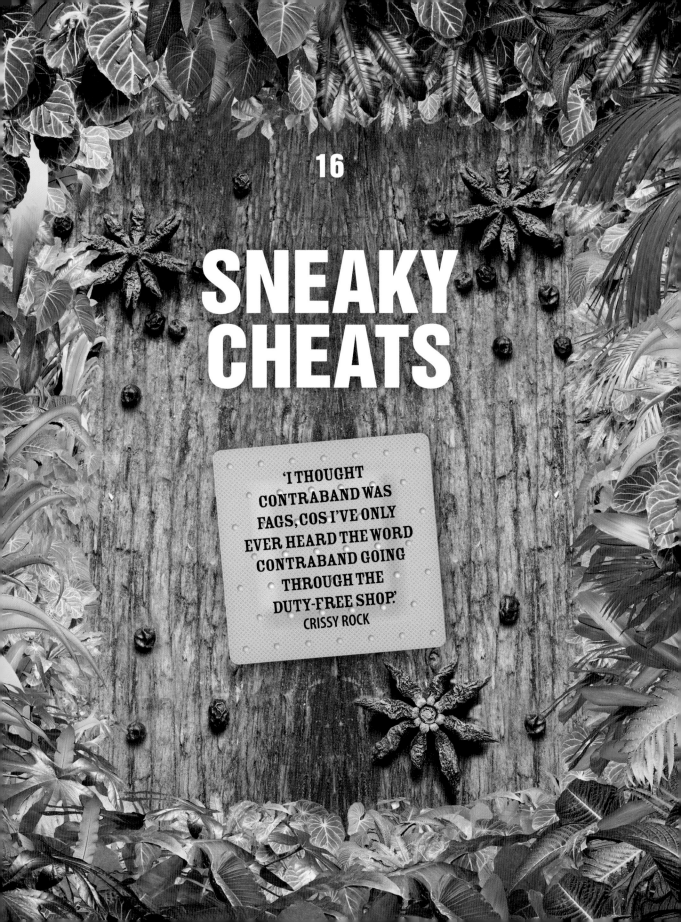

16

SNEAKY CHEATS

'I THOUGHT
CONTRABAND WAS
FAGS, COS I'VE ONLY
EVER HEARD THE WORD
CONTRABAND GOING
THROUGH THE
DUTY-FREE SHOP.'
CRISSY ROCK

EVERY YEAR, one or two celebrities choose not to play by the rules. Despite being told exactly what they can bring into camp (one luxury item, a toothbrush and three pairs of pants – we're not monsters), they try to smuggle in a load of contraband to improve their quality of life.

It's naughty, it's cheating, and it's probably best not to dwell for too long on exactly where they hide it – particularly if you're a fellow celebrity and that contraband is being sprinkled on your food.

The classic items smugglers bring in are salt, pepper and spices. You'd have to ask the campers where they hide that stuff – and you'd have to ask the other celebrities if where they hide that stuff affects the flavour.

The smugglers are invariably caught and told to hand over their booty, because however smart they are about getting it into camp, once it's in there they're absolutely rubbish at keeping it a secret.

Here are my top tips for future celebrity smugglers.

1. If you're wearing a microphone around your neck, whispering really loudly can actually be heard. What the producers do is TURN UP THE SOUND, you muppet.

2. When there's a hundred cameras pointing at you, holding your shirt over your hand while you pour a load of salt into a pot is remarkably easy to spot. What it looks like is a person holding their shirt over their hand while they pour a load of salt into a pot.

3. Doing lots of exaggerated over-the-top winking at anyone within fifty feet of you tends to attract the producers' attention.

Peppercorns and salt, smuggled in Jimmy Osmond's teddy bear

'EVERY YEAR SOMEONE TRIES TO SMUGGLE A BIT OF
CONTRABAND IN, AND GOD ARE YOU GRATEFUL FOR IT
WHEN YOU'RE IN THERE. I REMEMBER NOT EVEN HAVING
A CLUE THAT GILLIAN HAD ALL THIS STUFF.'
STACEY SOLOMON

MY SNEAKY SIX SMUGGLERS

Here's my sneaky six smugglers. It's worth noting that every last one of them got caught. Then again, maybe there's a load of amazing stuff we don't know about that people managed to hide from the producers for the entire three weeks.

Yeah, right.

1. Amy Willerton

Sitting pretty at number one, it has to be
Amy Willerton. In 2013, it wasn't so much
a question of what Amy had sneaked in, as
what wasn't in that bag of hers. Weirdly, Amy
called her bag Betsy. Or maybe she had a
person called Betsy living in there that she
was talking to.

I wouldn't put it past her.

Amy's bad behaviour had the whole camp
on her case after she missed not one but two
opportunities to come clean. I have no idea
how she got away with it for so long. After all, Amy seemed to have an entire
lingerie shop crammed into that bag, plus a range of cosmetics that would put
Boots to shame. The other celebrities are still moaning about it now.

2. Jimmy Osmond

Sneaking in at number two is little Jimmy Osmond. (He'll be thrilled: Jimmy hasn't been this high in the charts since 'Long Haired Lover From Liverpool' came out in 1974.)

Back in 2005, Jimmy was told off for smuggling in the usual stuff – salt and pepper. But what we later discovered was that Jimmy's luxury item, a giant teddy, had been cunningly customized before he set off for Australia. The teddy bear had been loaded up with salt and pepper, plus recorded messages from Jimmy's kids, telling Daddy that they loved him and missed him and all that mushy stuff. Jimmy would sneak off into the jungle to listen to the messages.

I think it's safe to say that this is the single most un-rock-and-roll thing a pop star has ever been caught doing. What is it with this guy? When he's on tour, does he check into hotels and tidy up the rooms?

Anyway, you'll be glad to know they took away Jimmy's teddy, tore its head off and chucked it in a skip. Okay, they didn't – they gave it back to him when he came out. Nobody ever does what I tell them on this show.

3. David Haye

At number three, it's heavyweight boxer David Haye. Now, unlike most people, David Haye seems to have a different phone for everything. There's one for his agent, one for the missus, one for his mates, one for his work … Someone should tell David you can actually dial different numbers on the same phone.

So anyway, David got busted in 2012 trying to smuggle in a load of his mobiles. The thing is, even if he'd got them into camp – how was he going to charge them?

Sometimes people just don't think things through.

4. Kim Woodburn

Kim Woodburn managed to smuggle a pair of sunglasses into camp in 2009 despite going through a thorough pat-down.

And yes, like you, I'm trying very hard not to picture where she hid them.

5. Gillian McKeith

Gillian McKeith takes the number five spot. Who will ever forget Gillian's amazing efforts back in 2010, when she managed to smuggle a load of herbs and spices into camp hidden in her knickers? I think, given the choice, I'd have taken my rice and beans bland.

> When Gillian left the jungle, she showed me these incredible pants. It turns out she'd had them made especially for the show. There were pockets sewn all over them. But even though they were mainly designed for smuggling, she still wore them.
>
> **Daisy Moore, Casting Executive**

6. Wayne Sleep

Waltzing in at number six is dancer Wayne Sleep, who tried to smuggle in a packet of Band-Aids. Yes, out of all the countless luxuries the celebrities were going to miss in the jungle, Wayne Sleep just couldn't bear the thought of three weeks without a plaster.

17

JUNGLE CHATS

'SOMEONE'S REPORTED ME, SAYING I'VE DEMEANED PARLIAMENT.'
NADINE DORRIES

'IF I'M EVER VOTING, I'LL THINK, I KNOW HER – SHE ATE OSTRICH'S ARSEHOLE ONE TIME.'
DAVID HAYE

THERE ARE MANY reasons to love *I'm A Celebrity … Get Me Out Of Here!* There's me, the Trials, Ant and Dec, me … But arguably the show's most memorable moments down the years have also been the most spontaneous – the conversations between celebrities who, without this show, would never have crossed paths in a million years.

There's something about seeing two famous people from completely different worlds squatting on a log and having a deep and meaningful conversation while their wet socks dangle on a stick behind them. Somehow, it makes whatever nonsense they're babbling on about seem so much more interesting.

And the beauty of sticking a load of celebrities in a camp miles away from civilization is that there's not a hell of a lot else to do in that camp but talk. Add to that the light-headedness that comes from the tiredness and hunger, and the fact that they're all going a little bit stir-crazy, and you never know what they might come out with.

So here, for your enjoyment, is a selection of just a few of the greatest quotes, comments, conversations, outbursts and general nonsense from the jungle vaults.

'ARGH! I JUST TOUCHED A TREE!'
NATALIE APPLETON

'IT'S MICHAEL JACKSON'S BIRTHDAY TODAY. AND WE'LL ALL WISH HIM WELL, SEND HIM TELEPATHICALLY HAPPY BIRTHDAY. WE WILL DRAW HERE A SYMBOL, PUT A TOWEL ON IT AND THEN FOR ABOUT ELEVEN MINUTES WE SHOULD SIT IN SILENCE AND BEAM THIS SIGNAL OUT … I THINK THAT MICHAEL IS RIGHT NOW IN TOUCH WITH ME. I KNOW HE'S SMILING. I THINK HE FEELS ME NOW. HE KNOWS THAT I'M OUT HERE.'
URI GELLER

(Sadly, Uri had got his dates mixed up. Michael Jackson's birthday was actually a day later.)

'IT'S CALLED "INSANIA". IT'S A MIXTURE OF INSANITY AND MANIA.'
PETER ANDRE

REBECCA ADLINGTON: I always pee in the pool.
JOEY ESSEX: You always pee in the pool?
REBECCA ADLINGTON: Everyone pees in the pool. You cannot get out from a swimming session.
JOEY ESSEX: You wee in the pool?

[Brian Harvey farts]
JANET STREET-PORTER: Hey, listen, don't do that when we're cooking, it's so inappropriate.
BRIAN HARVEY: Come off it, man!
JANET STREET-PORTER: No it's not, I'm sorry – I'm trying to cook dinner.
BRIAN HARVEY: We're outside, man, stop having a go at me for farting, for f**k's sake.
JANET STREET-PORTER: I'm trying to cook dinner, Brian, it's so——
BRIAN HARVEY: You're cooking dinner. You're over here. I'm over there. Don't keep having a go at me about farting. If I want to fart I'll f*****g fart. I'm nowhere near the f*****g food. We're outdoors, we're not cooped up in a small room.
JANET STREET-PORTER: Maybe you'd like to cook dinner tomorrow night and I'll come and fart in your face.
BRIAN HARVEY: I'm farting – cos I need to fart – cos all I've eaten is f*****g beans.

'BRIAN HARVEY NOT ONLY MOANED THE WHOLE TIME A WANTED MINERAL WATER, B AS I WAS COOKING HE FART IN MY FACE.'
JANET STREET-PORTER

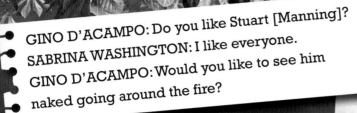

GINO D'ACAMPO: Do you like Stuart [Manning]?

SABRINA WASHINGTON: I like everyone.

GINO D'ACAMPO: Would you like to see him naked going around the fire?

'HE'S [JOHN BURTON RACE] THE ONE THAT WAS BEING BITCHY BY SAYING I WAS BEING BITCHY BY SAYING I WASN'T GOING TO BE BITCHY. BUT I WASN'T BEING BITCHY IN THE FIRST PLACE. HE'S BEING BITCHY.' LYNNE FRANKS

SHAUN RYDER: When I was a kid I used to climb everything. Those power things, you know – power cables. Pylons. Climb them. Climb anything. Loved getting chased. I loved climbing. I also enjoyed breaking and entering and vandalism. On our industrial estate, right, we had Schweppes, Bulmers … and by the time I was twelve I'd screwed the lot of them.

DOM JOLY: Screwed?

SHAUN RYDER: Robbed them all. I sold the booze to the ice-cream man; he went around then, selling booze. You know what someone once did as well, to me? Someone once broke into our junior school, chopped the heads off the hamsters and the guinea pigs, smashed the place to f**k and then wrote 'Shaun Ryder' on the blackboard. 'Shaun Ryder did this.' Spelt me name wrong, of course.

'WE MET NELSON MANDELA ON A BEACH IN MAURITIUS. OUT OF THE BLUE HE SAID, "YOU KNOW A FRIEND OF MINE." AND I LOOKED AT COLIN AND COLIN LOOKED AT ME AND HE SAID, "YOU KNOW CHARLIE DIMMOCK." NOW, CHARLIE DIMMOCK, FOR ANYBODY WHO DOESN'T KNOW, IS A GARDENER ON … SHE HAD A CALENDAR OUT … SHE NEVER WORE A BRA … AND HE WAS LIKE, "YEAH, SHE CAME OUT WITH HER PROGRAMME AND DID MY GARDEN." AND THEN HE SAID, "MY GARDEN'S LOOKING GREAT, BUT THE HOUSE LOOKS PRETTY MESSY – YOU SHOULD COME OUT AND TACKLE OUR HOUSE." ' JUSTIN RYAN

DOUGIE POYNTER: Didn't the capital of England used to be Colchester?
PAT SHARP: No, it's always been London.

By the way, apparently Dougie was correct about Colchester.

'IT'S CALLED SHOW BUSINESS, NOT SHOW FRIENDS.'
ANTONY COTTON

'DID I TELL YOU ABOUT THE TIME I HAD TEA WITH THE QUEEN?'
CHRISTOPHER BIGGINS

'HANG ON, HANG ON. WE'RE GOING TO GET AN ELECTRIC SHOCK, ARE WE? I DON'T DO THAT. I DON'T DO THAT. I'M LEAVING, OKAY, BECAUSE I DON'T DO ELECTRIC SHOCKS. UNTIL WE CAN SORT THAT OUT, I'M OUT OF HERE.'
NIGEL HAVERS

DOUGIE POYNTER: It's the drop bears you've got to worry about. They drop on your head and gnaw on your head and you've got to rip 'em off. Imagine: a little tiny bear thing … Oh, I just saw one!
MARK WRIGHT: What? What?
DOUGIE POYNTER: A drop bear.
MARK WRIGHT: Are you lying?
DOUGIE POYNTER: Mate, there's no such thing as drop bears.

'DO GIRLS HAVE A FAVOURITE BOOB?'
DOUGIE POYNTER TO JESSICA-JANE CLEMENT

18

THE WORLD ACCORDING TO BOB

'THERE'S A MAN CALLED MEDIC BOB. HE'S THE MAN WHO GIVES YOU ADVICE, WHO SORTS YOU OUT. SO I SAID, LIKE, "DR BOB, ANY TIPS, WHAT DO YOU RECKON?" AND HE SAID TO ME, "MAKE SURE YOU KILL THE COCKROACHES BEFORE YOU SWALLOW THEM, BECAUSE IF YOU SWALLOW THEM AND THEY'RE ALIVE, THEY'LL CRAWL BACK OUT OF YOUR DIGESTIVE SYSTEM." THAT'S DISGUSTING.'

JOE SWASH

ANYONE who's watched *I'm A Celebrity … Get Me Out Of Here!* will be familiar with the name Medic Bob. Bob plays a crucial role in the show. His job is to keep the celebrities alive and well so that you, the viewing public, can keep on starving and torturing them.

The celebrities love Bob. He's someone they can rely on. He's a shoulder to cry on. And he's got oxygen they can suck on.

Bob was born in London in the 1950s. His years of service as a paramedic in the community and for stage and film earned him the OAM (Order of Australia Medal). Bob's even worked on hit movies like *The Piano* and *The Matrix.*

But who is the man behind the myth?

Ladies and gentlemen. This is the World According to Bob.

A Day In The Life Of Medic Bob

I work five days a week for three months, looking after the crew as they put the show together. Then, just before the celebs arrive, I start working every day for seven weeks.

For me, there is no typical day. I usually begin at 6 a.m. and do a medical handover with my night-shift paramedic. My nurse arrives at the same time and then the two of us go over the Trials and challenges for the day. We have up to eight medical staff when we're doing Trials in remote locations. When I'm doing a Trial, I'm on set for about two hours.

We also work out if any of the celebrities need any medications or if I need to go into the jungle to see them.

We have approximately 600 people working on site and we treat an average of 30 cases a day in the clinic. It can be anything from leeches and tick bites, cut hands, thorns and splinters to people with ongoing medical issues such as diabetes, asthma or blood-pressure problems – the list is endless.

There are snake sightings pretty much every day. I've got a licence to catch snakes and then release them a safe distance from camp. I normally get home around 8 p.m., but then I'm on call throughout the night.

It's part of my job to help organize and pick out what we think the celebrities should eat if they're lucky enough to win some stars.

I'm always pulling ticks out of the celebrities, which again is quite serious, as some of them are paralysis ticks. I pulled one out of George Hamilton's butt. He was very proud – he went and showed it off to his campmates.

Another danger is that we've got branches falling from the trees all the time. In fact, when we did the show for the USA in 2009, a branch fell and hit a celebrity on the head in the middle of an interview, knocking him to the ground. It was all caught on camera.

Me And The Germans

I started on the very first show in July 2002 and I've been the medical supervisor ever since. I also work on the German version of the series, **Ich Bin Ein Star – Holt Mich Hier Raus!**

The German show is much tougher on the celebs when it comes to the Eating Trials. They make them eat and drink twice as much. The rations are also much less

appetizing than on the UK show. However, the German celebrities are only in the jungle for two weeks, rather than the three weeks the British celebs have to endure.

My Favourite Memories

I have so many memories from the show. The ones that stick out are: constantly carrying Gillian McKeith off the set after every fainting episode; watching Peter Andre trying to climb into Katie Price's bed in the dark, thinking that no one could see him; Janice Dickinson being bitten on the hand by a rat; and a certain female celeb taking a pee by a tree in the dark (we have infra-red cameras).

Being On Telly

The fame element has always surprised me. Before the UK show begins, my wife and I always head off on our holidays to Europe. When we're in the UK, I have many people coming up and asking 'Are you Medic Bob from **I'm A Celebrity**?'

On one occasion, I was with my wife on a small fishing boat just off the island of Iona in Scotland. There we were, bobbing along on the sea with about twenty other tourists. Then two of them recognized me – and word spread right across the rest of the boat. So here we were, miles from civilization up in Scotland, with people asking me about the job I do in Australia.

I'm always being asked to have a photo taken with people – mostly by German tourists, but also Brits. I've been walking through Hanoi airport in Vietnam, Bangkok airport, even Seoul in South Korea and people have come up to me.

It always takes me by surprise. I've no idea how people recognize me when I'm not in my uniform.

In Germany I'm very well known. I was once asked to join a group of celebrities on a TV show in Berlin. When I arrived at the airport, even the customs official recognized me!

I've even had a single out in Germany based on stuff I say on the show.

My Favourite Trial

My favourite Trial was the Live Trial with Dean Gaffney. Live Trials are particularly difficult – I've got to be ready for any potential problem, such as a bad bite from a snake, or a celebrity fainting or going into a full panic attack.

But with Dean, I had trouble keeping the tears from my eyes – we were all in hysterics!

I particularly like the Trials that end up with the celebs covered in cockroaches, worms, slime and feathers. They always look so shell-shocked when it's over. I tell them to go back into camp as they are and not to clean up on the way. That way they get lots of sympathy, praise and congratulations from their teammates – they're like gladiators returning from battle.

My Most Challenging Celebrities

Janice Dickinson was my most challenging celebrity. Janice demanded to talk to me every single day. Every time she did a Trial she was looking for me and every time she went to the Bush Telegraph she was asking to see me.

I had my work cut out with Gillian McKeith, too. She fainted almost every time she did a Trial. Loads of people think she was faking, but when a celeb drops to the floor seemingly unconscious, I have to take it seriously. The possible problems are serious.

What I Say To The Stars

During my first meeting with the celebrities at their hotels, when I perform my medical checks and give them an idea of what life in camp is all about, I do tell them that anything I say to them on or off camera is the truth.

Both ethically and personally, they need to know I would never lie to them. However, this does not stop me from making them feel nervous before the Trials. I also give them a few tips on where and when it might not be good to look up with an open mouth, and to be when you put your hand into a dark hole, don't rush in and out, but move slowly and gently.

My First Appearance

When we did the first series in 2002, Nigel Benn was bitten on the back of the hand by a python. Ant and Dec had a panicked look on their faces and asked me to step in to check Nigel out.

Nigel was grasping his hand and looking like he was about to drop. This was my first time on camera for the show and afterwards the producers asked me if I could go on camera and talk to the celebs about the Trials.

At that mo

MEDICAL
DEPARTMENT

PLEASE KNOCK
THEN WAIT
THANK YOU

I was walking down to social [the catering area]. It's a steep slope and I slipped and fell over for the second time in two days at the same stretch of road. It hurt me in exactly the same spot as well. I headed straight to Medic Bob's office on the verge of tears, and he handed me a Chupa Chups lolly. Bob always has a stash of sweets on hand. He's good like that.

Helen Kruger-Bratt, Production Executive

179

19

FAVOURITE MOMENTS

'IT'S THE MOST WONDERFUL THING I'VE DONE IN MY ENTIRE LIFE. IT'S JUST A MAGICAL PLACE.'
TONY BLACKBURN

LOOK, I'M NOT PROUD. And I'm prepared to accept that for a good 15–20 per cent of the public, Brucey the Cockroach is not the only reason to watch *I'm A Celebrity ... Get Me Out Of Here!*
I accept that. I don't understand it. But I accept it.
My point is that we've all got our favourite moments from down the years and some of them don't feature me. Here are just a few of my personal favourites.

RHONA CAMERON'S 'SOMETIMES...' SPEECH (series 1)

'DARREN SAID, "SOMETIMES I FIND YOU SARCASTIC AND PATRONIZING." AND I JUST FELT LIKE GOING, "F**K'S SAKE, YOU KNOW, YES, I AM. THAT'S REALLY BAD. SOMETIMES I AM." THEN I JUST STARTED TO PICK UP OTHER PEOPLE'S PERHAPS MORE DIFFICULT TRAITS.'
RHONA CAMERON

For many viewers, the ongoing love affair with *I'm A Celebrity ... Get Me Out Of Here!* can be traced right back to one unforgettable moment: the day Rhona Cameron stood up and took the rest of the camp apart with one lethally targeted speech.

It was right then that people realized just how much the show had to offer.

Rhona's probably dined out on that speech ever since.

Short, sweet and straight to the point, it doesn't get better than this.

RHONA CAMERON: Darren, sometimes you behave like a twat.

DARREN DAY: Oh. Okay ...

RHONA CAMERON: Sometimes I'm patronizing. Sometimes I'm sarcastic. Sometimes he's hot-headed. Sometimes Nell says nothing. Sometimes Uri dramatizes little things like a fart like he's an alien just landed who's never seen it before. Sometimes Tony misses things because he's slightly slower. Sometimes Tara is like a child who's never been able to make a cup of tea. Sometimes, sometimes, sometimes, we're all like that.

'LOOKING BACK AT IT, IT'S SLIGHTLY INSULTING.'
TONY BLACKBURN

TIMMY MALLETT'S LAST STAND
(series 8)

Sometimes there are classic moments that make it all worthwhile. There's no particular reason they're classic, but somehow they just stick in the mind.

The Last Chance Saloon Trial was one of those moments.

To set the scene: Timmy Mallett and Brian Paddick are going head-to-head in a do-or-die Trial. The winner stays in camp, the loser leaves forever.

Ant and Dec explain the Trial is called Last Chance Saloon. As Ant explains what Timmy and Brian have to do, you can see the truth dawning on Timmy's face. For the first time in his life, he's speechless; but Timmy's eyes tell you everything you need to know.

Because it's an Eating Trial. And Timmy Mallett is a vegetarian. He really, really wants to stay on the show. But he really, really doesn't want to be doing this.

While Brian's talking about what the Trial means to him, Timmy's nervously ripping bits of paper into tiny pieces. He tries to put a brave face on it, but there's no hiding the terror and repulsion he's feeling right now.

To Timmy's credit, he gives it his best shot. But having to leave the camp like that must have left a bad taste in his mouth.

A very, very bad taste indeed.

Here's what the Trial involved:

ROUND ONE

Beetlejuice cocktails: cockroaches and mealworms with a sprinkling of darkling beetles to serve. Brian edges the first round. 1–0.

ROUND TWO

Leafcutter ant and Mopani worms: Timmy finally manages to get them down. 1–1.

ROUND THREE

Penis colada: a blend of crocodile and camel penis.

Once again it's a close contest, a battle that leaves Timmy with what Dec describes as a 'penis moustache'. The look on Timmy's face when Dec tells him this is beyond description. Put it this way: he's not laughing any more. 2–1 to Brian.

ROUND FOUR

Tesquealer: sand worms served in clear liquid.

And it's all over, despite Timmy's attempts to put Brian off by grabbing and squeezing his arm. The moment Timmy knows he's lost, he spits out the sand worms. 3–1 to Brian.

Brian shows Timmy the mark on his arm, but Timmy's beyond caring – he looks distraught as Brian is declared the winner. There's not much clowning left in Timmy. What is in him is a pint of camel and croc penis smoothie.

A classic Bushtucker Trial and a moment of genuine TV gold.

STACEY THROWS STONE AT DOM (series 10)

'TODAY'S DAY TWO OF MY SECRET MISSION AND I HAD TO ATTRACT DOM'S ATTENTION TO GET HIM INTO THE BUSH TELEGRAPH WITHOUT ANYONE NOTICING. SUBTLE IS MY MIDDLE NAME.' STACEY SOLOMON

It was over in a second, but it was a series-defining moment.

Stacey's been given a secret mission. She needs to get Dom into the Bush Telegraph. So how does she choose to do it? By throwing a stone right in his face, of course. Comedy gold.

> JENNY ECLAIR: Did it sting?
> DOM JOLY: No, but it was like someone threw a rock in my face.

CRISSY ROCK FORGETS HER TEETH
(series 11)

When a celebrity makes their way into the jungle, they've got a lot on their mind. Did I turn the boiler off? Did I lock the front door when I left home? Have I brought my teeth?

For Crissy Rock back in 2011, the answer to that final question was no.

So Crissy Rock was one of a group due to do the skydive. Antony Cotton was in uproar – we thought he'd be the one not to do it. Crissy looked all gung-ho, like she was right up for it, no worries at all.

However, Crissy does wear false teeth.

For safety reasons, she wasn't allowed to jump with her teeth in. After all, if they fall out at 12,000 feet we're never going to find them.

So, Lorraine Chase landed – all fine; then someone else landed – all fine. Then it was meant to be Crissy. But instead Antony landed and we're like – what? Where's Crissy?

Then we heard the pilot saying, 'This one's not gonna jump, mate, we're going to return to the last location.'

So the helicopter went off and we're thinking it would be a good story – Crissy won't jump. And we had a producer waiting for her chopper to land so they could interview her as soon as she lands.

So we're organizing it all when at the same time Chris Elliot, the Head of Safety, and I looked at each other and we both went, 'We've got her teeth!'

Because we'd brought her teeth with us to the drop zone so that when she landed we could give them back to her.

And all we could think of was this crew and a producer were back where she was supposed to land ready to interview her and she wouldn't be able to talk! So we had to call in a helicopter to fly in, collect her teeth and take them over to her. Next thing two helicopters came flying in. One was picking up the teeth. The other was filming the first one!

So the teeth were flown very expensively back to be reunited with their owner.

Becca Walker, Executive Producer

JANICE DICKINSON'S STAKEOUT TRIAL (series 7)

ANT: Once you're in and you're tied down, five boxes full of critters will be dumped on you.
JANICE DICKINSON: Get the f**k
ANT: Let me finish, Janice, before you start swearing.

She'd flirted with Dec, she'd fought with Lynne Franks. She went on to appear in the second US series. But for me, Janice Dickinson's greatest moment, and one of my favourite ever moments, is when she took on the Stakeout Trial in the final show of the series back in 2007.

Suffice to say, she expressed herself freely.

Janice was brilliant. She just played the game. I heard she had a tummy tuck especially for going into the jungle. Mind you, I think any time she's doing a show she probably has a bit of work done.

Natalka Znak, Executive Producer and Co-Creator

ANT: Does it smell?
JANICE DICKINSON: I had two babies. You think placenta smells, you jerk-off! Are you kidding me?
DEC: That's good, Janice, you're in the zone.
JANICE DICKINSON: I'm not in the zone!

20

FAQs

'AS YOU'VE PROBABLY NOTICED, ONE OF THE
MAIN METHODS OF COMMUNICATION IN THE
JUNGLE IS THE LAMINATED CARD. IT'S BASICALLY
THE EQUIVALENT OF A JUNGLE EMAIL.'
DEC

I'm A Celebrity … Get Me Out Of Here! is one of those shows that gets people talking. At home, at work, in the pub – and these days, on social media too.

There are all sorts of forums, threads and blogs burbling away when the show hits the air. Now, I'll be honest. I don't really get involved with any of that stuff – computers, tweeting and all that. Mainly because I DON'T HAVE ANY HANDS!!!

And just in case you're wondering how I've managed to write a book, a PA is transcribing every word I say.

She's middle-aged. She's a bit frumpy-looking. She's got a mole on her upper lip.

She's … giving me the stink-eye right now.

She's also the third PA I've hired so far. They never last long. Apparently I'm difficult to work with. Please! If swearing, shouting, throwing crockery around and ordering five Manhattans at 3.30 a.m. before downing them and sobbing with self-loathing is 'difficult', then aren't we all?

Anyway, like I said, every year there are thousands of people who go online to talk about the show, and quite a few of them post questions. So I thought I'd stick some of those questions in front of the experts to see if they can come up with the definitive answers.

Q: How are celebrities picked?

A: Every year there's a long casting process where we'll meet anywhere between sixty and ninety potential celebrities.

David Harvey, Casting Executive

Q: Is the shower water hot or cold?

A: Very cold.

Richard Cowles, Executive Producer and Co-Creator

Q: Is there a reserve list in case a celebrity is taken ill?

A: Yes, but not always. We sometimes have standbys in Australia, or ready to get on a plane at a moment's notice. We only have them standing by until the vote-offs begin, as we wouldn't put anyone in after that.

Richard Cowles, Executive Producer and Co-Creator

Q: Do the celebrities know who else is in the show before they enter?

A: No. We keep them in separate hotels after they arrive in Australia.

Richard Cowles, Executive Producer and Co-Creator

Q: Do Ant and Dec watch the series?

A: Eh? You can actually watch them watching the series. They can't watch it when they're doing their links. Because they're busy doing their links! Some of these questions are raising my blood pressure.

Brucey

Q: During filming in Australia, does everyone work on UK time or Australian time?

A: It's a mix. The site runs twenty-four hours a day when the show is on air, so some people are working on British time and some are on Aussie time.

Richard Cowles, Executive Producer and Co-Creator

Q: What time is it in Australia when the show is on TV?

A: It says the time in Australia on a clock on your screen. I mean, it's actually right there on your TV screen. Right there. On your screen!

Brucey

Q: What happens to the camp after the show has ended?

A: Once the UK and German shows have finished, the camp, studio and surrounding areas are put into 'hibernation' until we come back and start preparations for the next series.

Richard Cowles, Executive Producer and Co-Creator

Q: Do the celebrities leave the camp during the night to sleep in a hotel?

A: Hang on – I'll take this one. Yes. Absolutely. We stop all the cameras, take them to a posh hotel, bathe them in goat's milk, give them a slap-up dinner and put them to bed in silk sheets. Then every morning we get them up early, rush them back to the jungle, rub them in filth, drag them through a bush backwards and stick them on a log for the live show. Does that answer your question?

Brucey

Q: Any plans for a winners' series, with all previous winners re-entering the jungle?

A: It has often been suggested, but for me, the fascination of I'm A Celebrity is watching people who've never been in the jungle – getting to know them and then seeing how they cope with it. Never say never, though!

Richard Cowles, Executive Producer and Co-Creator

Q: Do celebrities get to speak with their agents?

A: No. They get a phone call at the hotel before they go in and that's it.

David Harvey, Casting Executive

Q: Do Ant and Dec write their own scripts?

A: Ant and Dec work with their writers, Andy Milligan and Mark Busk-Cowley, to put together the scripts.

Richard Cowles, Executive Producer and Co-Creator

Q: Is there a nurse in the camp?

A: Better than that: there's Medic Bob. Plus a medical team (that includes a nurse) on call twenty-four hours when the series is on.

Richard Cowles, Executive Producer and Co-Creator

Q: How long after the show has ended does everyone stay around?

A: For many people, their role on the show finishes when the final show transmits. There's a big wrap party on the evening that follows the final show where the crew and the celebrities all let their hair down. Then they either head for home or take a holiday in Australia. The technical suppliers stick around a bit longer for what we call de-rig, when all the equipment is dismantled – the cameras, editing suites, etc. – but only a few weeks after that, in early January, the German show begins setting up.

Richard Cowles, Executive Producer and Co-Creator

Q: Is there a time delay from when the show is being seen in the UK compared to when it's filmed in Australia?

A: The show is transmitted live, but since John Lydon decided to say a very rude word live on air, there is a deliberate five-second delay in place. In terms of filming the content of each show, because Australia is ten hours ahead, when the show transmits at 9 p.m. in the UK, it's 7 a.m. the next day in Australia. So at the end of each show, when most people in the UK are thinking about going to bed, it's daytime in Australia and we start filming and editing the content for the next day's show.

Richard Cowles, Executive Producer and Co-Creator

Q: When do Ant and Dec travel to the jungle?

A: Ant and Dec normally arrive just over a week before the first show. They do a rehearsal show with stand-ins, to make sure everything is working properly. We use Australians – they pretend to be the celebrities. They stay in the camp for about three days. They do Trials, they eat all the same food. It's a very weird experience for them.

Richard Cowles, Executive Producer and Co-Creator

Q: How many people work on the Trials?

A: Lots! There is a Trials Series Producer and Series Director. Two Trials Producers, one Associate Producer, a dedicated Production Manager and Co-ordinator, as well as teams for art, animals and cameras. Around twenty-five people in all.

Richard Cowles, Executive Producer and Co-Creator

Q: Whereabouts in Australia is the camp?

A: It's on the border between New South Wales and Queensland and about an hour inland from the coast, in a place called Dungay Creek.

Richard Cowles, Executive Producer and Co-Creator

Q: The highlights we see on TV – when were they filmed?

A: The VTs you see are from the day before. This is one of the reasons we film in Australia. Because we're ten hours ahead, when the celebrities are sleeping, we're editing the show together. Then, when they wake up, the show is just coming to an end in the UK and Ant and Dec are walking into the camp. So basically, when you watch the programme at home, you're seeing everything that's happened up until the celebrities went to bed.

Richard Cowles, Executive Producer and Co-Creator

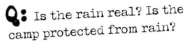

NAME

Q: Is the rain real? Is the camp protected from rain?

A: There's a canopy over the camp to stop it getting rained on directly, which would put the fire out. It's really high up – about fifty feet. But that's it. Camp isn't a great place to be in the rain; often water runs straight through the camp when you get a proper downpour.
Richard Cowles, Executive Producer and Co-Creator

Q: How much footage is filmed compared to what's shown on TV?

A: There are over fifty cameras shooting around the clock. That's all edited down to around thirty minutes of VTs for a one-hour show.
Richard Cowles, Executive Producer and Co-Creator

Q: When the celebrities win a Trial, who decides what food they are going to get?

A: We have a set number of meals that we pre-plan to put in during the run, and that is tweaked according to how many stars the celebrities have won. The exact meal they get is decided by the senior producer on site and Medic Bob.
Richard Cowles, Executive Producer and Co-Creator

Q: Is there a list of things the celebrities can't take in with them?

A: Yes. It's a very long list. The only personal belongings the celebrities can take into camp are three sets of underwear and three sets of swimwear – we provide everything else. The celebrities can take in one luxury item. The luxury item can't be anything that would stop them interacting with the group – so no books, iPods, computers etc. The most popular luxury items are pillows, chairs and photographs.
Richard Cowles, Executive Producer and Co-Creator

Q: Does Father Christmas visit the camp at Christmas?

A: I don't know. We've all left by then.

Brucey

Q: How far is the camp from the nearest city and what is the city?

A: The nearest city is Brisbane, which is about a ninety-minute drive. That's also where most of the celebrities fly into.

Richard Cowles, Executive Producer and Co-Creator

Q: Is there a security fence around the whole jungle set? Can anyone walk in?

A: There's not a security fence, but there is thick rainforest. And hiding all through that rainforest are our highly skilled security team. These guys are good. They could be five feet from you and you wouldn't have a clue. There's a couple of them near the camp at all times and the celebrities don't suspect a thing. They're there to prevent venomous snakes getting into camp. Of course, they can't catch them all, so there have been some hair-raising moments over the years. Very occasionally, paparazzi have tried to sneak into the site. They always get caught.

Richard Cowles, Executive Producer and Co-Creator

Q: Is there a gym in the camp? David Hayes was using something in 2012.

A: We change camp around each year. In 2012 there was a gym; some very senior female producers thought it would be wrong for David not to be able to work out - and for viewers (and them) not to be able to watch!

Richard Cowles, Executive Producer and Co-Creator

Q: Where is the ITV2 set?

A: It's the same studio the main show uses. They move in the moment the main show finishes.

Richard Cowles, Executive Producer and Co-Creator

Q: What's the temperature?

A: It's getting into summer when the show goes on air, so it can get very warm and humid in the rainforest. The temperatures can get into the high 30s.

Richard Cowles, Executive Producer and Co-Creator

Q: What time do the celebrities wake up in the morning?

A: The first few days they don't sleep that much. Once they've settled in, it's usually around 6 a.m. local time. In week one, Ant and Dec go in there live at around 7.50 a.m., so they need to be up and ready for that.

Richard Cowles, Executive Producer and Co-Creator

Q: Where did the idea for *I'm A Celebrity* come from?

A: The show was in development for a number of years before it was commissioned. I think the man responsible for the title was Brent Baker, one of the early developers of the show. He gave it the working title 'Get Me Out of Here – I'm a Celebrity!' But it was later decided that it worked better the other way round.

Richard Cowles, Executive Producer and Co-Creator

Q: Do celebrities have to be able to swim to take part in the show?

A: No. For example, Simon Webbe had to do a Trial in the pool, which came as a shock to him because he could barely swim.

Richard Cowles, Executive Producer and Co-Creator

Q: Is it real champagne the celebrities drink when they are being interviewed after they leave?

A: Yes, the celebrities are given the choice of the champagne or a soft drink.

Richard Cowles, Executive Producer and Co-Creator

Q: Is there a clock in camp?

A: No. We work very hard to make sure the celebrities have no way of telling the time. Whenever Ant and Dec or any crew members are near the celebrities they wear covers over their watches. We don't want the cast to have any idea what time it is - it's all part of making them feel like they're completely detached from the world.

Richard Cowles, Executive Producer and Co-Creator

Q: Is there shampoo in the shower?

A: Yes, there is a chest in camp that provides celebrities with everything they need for washing, but, because of the sensitive environment, it all has to be biodegradable.

Richard Cowles, Executive Producer and Co-Creator

Q: Is there any animal or insect which has been featured in every series?

A: Yes. Me. And I'm slightly offended you had to ask.

Brucey

Q: Who owns the land where the show is made?

A: The show is filmed on two adjoining properties that are privately owned.

Richard Cowles, Executive Producer and Co-Creator

Q: Why is it filmed in November? What's the weather like during other months of the year?

A: We film in November because that's when ITV want the show to be on. If it was on at another time of the year, we might have to move location, because there is a rainy season that would make working impossible.

Richard Cowles, Executive Producer and Co-Creator

21

THE KINGS AND QUEENS

'PEOPLE THINK YOU'VE GOT TO BE A VILLAIN. IT'S USUALLY THE GOOD ONES THAT COME THROUGH.'
PETER ANDRE

STRIP AWAY the fear, the hunger, the misery and the acts of mindless cruelty and *I'm A Celebrity … Get Me Out Of Here!* is at heart a popularity contest, in which ultimately the public vote for the celeb they like best. Or at least, the celeb they can still bear, after having them blabbing away in their living rooms for three weeks. Which means that, when the show comes to an end and the celebrities return home to appear on *Loose Women* and sofa adverts, one person will take with them a very special title.

And when I say 'very special', I mean 'completely made up'.

Yes, there's no other show on telly that brilliantly manages to avoid giving away any prize money by instead handing over a crown made of twigs and leaves, a reasonably big stick and the chance to sit in an uncomfortable chair for ten minutes before you get to meet your family.

In case you hadn't guessed it, I'm talking about the annual crowning of the King or Queen of the Jungle.

Every year, one person walks away with this prestigious title, as chosen by the viewers of the show.

You might not know it, but being crowned King or Queen of the Jungle is a lifetime honour. Which means our Kings and Queens never lose the complete lack of privileges that come with the title.

Over the years we've had old winners, young winners, boys and girls, everyone from soap stars to pop stars to an ex-prime minister's daughter.

I don't think it's an exaggeration to say that becoming King or Queen of the Jungle is the single greatest honour that can be won in any jungle-based celebrity reality TV show.

Traditionally, the King or Queen's main duties are to appear in several Iceland adverts during the following twelve months and to do some panto.

Here's my official roll call of the Kings and Queens we've loved over the years.

'THE WINNERS ARE PEOPLE THAT THE PUBLIC REALLY TAKE TO THEIR HEARTS. YOU DON'T GET ANY REALLY UNPLEASANT PEOPLE.'
JANET STREET-PORTER

TONY BLACKBURN,
Series 1

'I SAID TO MY WIFE: I'M GOING OUT TO AUSTRALIA TO LIVE WITH A LOAD OF CELEBRITIES OUT IN THE JUNGLE FOR A FORTNIGHT. AND SHE SAID: NO YOU'RE NOT.'
TONY BLACKBURN

'MY FAVOURITE KING HAS TO GO RIGHT BACK TO THE ORIGINAL SHOW – IT'S TONY BLACKBURN.'
DAVID VAN DAY

The first ever series of *I'm A Celebrity … Get Me Out Of Here!* was a non-stop bunfight.

Nigel Benn fell out with Rhona Cameron. Then Nigel fell out with Christine Hamilton. Then Darren Day fell out with Tara Palmer-Tomkinson. Then Darren fell out with Rhona.

Then, to save time, Rhona delivered her 'Sometimes …' speech, which insulted everybody at once.

In the midst of all the bickering and sniping, Tony Blackburn lived in his own little world – a world where he could talk to logs.

'I LOVE THE FACT THAT TONY GOT INTO A RELATIONSHIP WITH HIS LOGS.'
CHRISTOPHER BIGGINS

'HELLO, LOGS. HOW ARE YOU? LOVELY TO SEE YOU.'
TONY BLACKBURN

Tony Blackburn was the quiet achiever. Right up to the final day he was telling me there was no way he could win. On the last day I spoke to him – he said he'd be delighted for Tara to take the crown, but during that final Trial I could see a quiet determination on his face.

Medic Bob

Tony created the template for all future winners. It's not rocket science. It pretty much goes like this: behave like a decent human being with a sense of humour and you're in with a shout of going all the way.

I remember when Tony Blackburn and Tara Palmer-Tomkinson suddenly realized they were the last two celebrities in camp. It was more than a day before the winner was revealed.

Now, with this being the first series, the producers haven't planned a great deal for them to do. Tony and Tara really haven't spoken much up until this point. And they still don't have much to say to each other now they're stuck in camp on their own.

So for twenty-four long hours the two of them just sit around on their logs, staring into the distance and looking a bit awkward. It was hilarious, like watching a teenager being trapped in a lift with a grown-up they don't really know. I loved every minute.

'I THINK BECAUSE HE WAS THE FIRST KING OF THE JUNGLE, HE WILL ALWAYS REMAIN THE BEST.'
CHRISTOPHER BIGGINS

'WHEN TONY WENT INTO THE JUNGLE YOU WOULDN'T HAVE GIVEN HIM A CHANCE, BUT EVERYBODY TOOK HIM TO THEIR HEARTS.'
JANET STREET-PORTER

When the last programme finished and Tony had been crowned King, he spent a bit of time packing his rucksack up. Most people had gone to the catering tent. I was in the satellite truck feeding material back for the news and came out to find Tony standing on his own at the top of the ramp looking completely bewildered. I ran over and congratulated him and Tony just said, 'Are those generators?' The scale of the show was completely unknown to them.

Jane Smith, Production Executive

PHIL TUFNELL,
series 2

In the second series of *I'm A Celebrity … Get Me Out Of Here!*, Phil Tufnell cemented his reputation as an all-round okay geezer.

His tactic? Well, he basically sat around smoking his fags and having a bit of a laugh while the rest of the camp got themselves all wound up about the size of their sausage portions.

Good lad.

'EVERYONE LOVES PHIL. TUFFERS IS THE MAN.'
JOE SWASH

'I CAN REMEMBER ASKING LINDA TO MAKE SURE THAT I DIDN'T LOSE THE PLOT COMPLETELY.'
PHIL TUFNELL

'YOU AIN'T GOT ANY FAGS, HAVE YOU? NO ONE'S GOT ANY FAGS. FAGS MAN. TELL HIM I'LL GIVE HIM FIVE HUNDRED QUID FOR FIVE FAGS.'
PHIL TUFNELL

KERRY KATONA,
series 3

'THE WHOLE JUNGLE EXPERIENCE WAS PHENOMENAL AND I'D GO BACK IN A HEARTBEAT.'
KERRY KATONA

Kerry Katona was your classic jungle surprise package. When Kerry first went into camp, the public didn't have much time for her. Not surprising, really. After all, Kerry looked like she was going to be just another one of those pampered celebrities who screams a lot and doesn't get their hands dirty.

But then she was chosen to face a Bushtucker Trial called Jungle Houdini. Nobody thought she stood a chance. And in the end she only got two stars. But what mattered was Kerry gave it a go, and from that moment on her popularity grew by the day.

Kerry won people over, both in and out of the camp.

'I'M A WOMAN. A VOLUMPTIOUS WOMAN ...'
KERRY KATONA

JOE PASQUALE, series 4

Towards the end of 2004, Joe Pasquale was having a nightmare.

Almost from the moment they arrived, model Sophie Anderton and singer Natalie Appleton were at each other's throats. And when Joe tried to step in and calm things down, they turned on him.

In the end, Joe decided enough was enough. He ended up spending most of his time outside camp with a couple of baby emus. Two noisy birds, squawking and screeching all day long – yes, Natalie and Sophie were some of the worst-behaved celebs I can remember.

Anyway, Joe and the emus became the stars of series 4, and Joe got his hands on the crown.

'JOE PASQUALE WAS A PROPER GENTLEMAN AND A GENUINELY FUNNY BLOKE.'
MEDIC BOB

CAROL THATCHER, series 5

'DID I EVER THINK I'D BE WELL KNOWN FOR CHEWING MY WAY THROUGH A KANGAROO BALL ON *I'M A CELEBRITY*? NO. BUT EVERYBODY TOLD ME THAT THE WHOLE BUSHTUCKER TRIAL LOOKED LIKE WE WERE HAVING TEA AT THE RITZ.'
CAROL THATCHER

As we all know, the winner of *I'm A Celebrity … Get Me Out Of Here!* is always the last to go.

Except, that is, for Carol Thatcher. In 2005, Carol was the first to go – she went right there on the ground next to her bed the night she arrived in camp, the dirty devil.

Carol didn't tell anybody what she'd been up to. So when a note arrived in camp telling the celebrities to stop weeing in the jungle, everyone was left asking one question: who was the guilty party?

SID OWEN: I'm pretty sure it weren't me.
JILLY GOOLDEN: No, but you can't have done it, Sid. Why are you having this paranoia?
JIMMY OSMOND: Now you've got me thinking … like, maybe I did it.

Classic stuff. Of course, Carol was crowned Queen three weeks later, making it the royal wee! Badum-tish! I thank you.

MATT WILLIS, series 6

'I WAS FLABBERGASTED. I WAS REALLY TAKEN ABACK BY IT. I COULDN'T BELIEVE THAT PEOPLE HAD VOTED FOR ME TO WIN.'
MATT WILLIS

While a lively camp including David Gest, Dean Gaffney and Jason Donovan hogged the headlines in 2006, former Busted singer Matt quietly charmed his way into the final.

Nobody had him down as a potential winner. But they hadn't bargained for a last, epic Bushtucker Trial.

It was the year a brand-new delicacy appeared on the menu: kangaroo anus. And with one eye-watering bite of Skippy's backside, Matt Willis carved his name on the jungle crown.

> 'EVEN IF YOU CAN EAT A KANGAROO ANUS, IT DOESN'T MEAN YOU'RE SUPPOSED TO.'
> MATT WILLIS

CHRISTOPHER BIGGINS,
series 7

Biggins. What a legend.

From the second he entered camp, Biggins was nothing less than a force of nature.

For me, his defining moment was when he recruited the entire camp to play a game of Filthy Charades. It turned out Biggins was only doing it to make the celebrities shout out a load of dirty words.

I love Biggins.

> 'IF I HAD COME FOURTH, LIKE DAVID GEST DID THE PREVIOUS YEAR, I'D HAVE BEEN VERY HAPPY.'
> CHRISTOPHER BIGGINS

Without a doubt, Biggins was my favourite celebrity that year. My favourite moment on the show was when he walked into the Bush Telegraph, raised his arms and asked for a new pair of trousers. The ones he was wearing dropped to the floor – Biggins had lost 15 kilos that year!

Medic Bob

JOE SWASH,
series 8

'THE JUNGLE EXPERIENCE WAS AMAZING. I WOULDN'T CHANGE IT
FOR THE WORLD. BUT THERE WERE TIMES WHEN IT WAS TOUGH.'
JOE SWASH

Joe Swash has turned his trip to the jungle into a whole new career as host of
ITV2's *I'm A Celebrity … Get Me Out Of Here! NOW!*

Joe's a pleasure to work with, a genuinely decent bloke, and it was that quality
that shone through back in 2008. While the rest of the campmates were turning on
new arrivals David Van Day and Timmy Mallett, Joe was the only one prepared to
stick up for them.

For that gesture alone, Joe deserved to win.

Joe now tries out most of the new Bushtucker Trials, so we spend a lot of time
together. He's godfather to several hundred of my kids.

'SOMETIMES IT CAN BE REALLY NASTY AND YOU CAN HAVE REALLY LOW TIMES IN CAMP. IT WAS REALLY SAD TO SEE A GROUP OF PEOPLE ATTACK TWO OTHER PEOPLE WHO HAD JUST ARRIVED. IT JUST FELT LIKE IT WAS TOO MUCH IN THERE AND I HAD TO STAND UP FOR THEM. THEY HADN'T DONE ANYTHING WRONG. PROBABLY ONE OF THE LOWEST POINTS WAS THAT. BUT ONE OF THE HIGHEST POINTS WAS STANDING UP FOR THEM, I FELT GOOD ABOUT MYSELF. THEY WERE TWO LOVELY FELLAS WHO HAD COME FOR AN EXPERIENCE AND IT WAS BEING SPOILED BY OTHER PEOPLE.'
JOE SWASH

'I'VE NEVER WON ANYTHING IN MY LIFE – I'M JOE SWASH. I DON'T WIN ANYTHING. AND THE ONE THING I WIN WAS THE MOST AMAZING EXPERIENCE OF MY LIFE – WAS THE JUNGLE.'
JOE SWASH

GINO D'ACAMPO, series 9

'THERE'S ONLY ONE THING THAT MAKES YOU KING OR QUEEN OF THE JUNGLE. IT'S BEING A GOOD MAN. IF YOU'RE A GOOD PERSON, YOU WILL GO A LONG WAY.'
GINO D'ACAMPO

There's always room for a good chef in the jungle. Someone who can take the assorted animal parts that arrive in the Flying Fox and turn them into something edible. So Gino was always in for a warm welcome.

But what really sealed the deal for Gino was his boundless energy and sense of humour.

I'll never forget the sight of Gino slurping up a forkful of beach worms and trying to convince himself it was a delicious mouthful of spaghetti.

That really wasn't the way Mamma used to make it.

STACEY SOLOMON,
series 10

'I THINK IN LIFE IN GENERAL YOU JUST HAVE TO BE HONEST AND WHO YOU ARE, SO I SUPPOSE IT MUST APPLY IN THE JUNGLE AS WELL.'
STACEY SOLOMON

'SHE'S NOT JUST A NUTTY BIRD, YOU KNOW – SHE'S A REALLY CLEVER YOUNG WOMAN.'
SHAUN RYDER

'STACEY SOLOMON REALLY SURPRISED ME. SHE HAD A LITTLE BIT OF FIGHT IN HER.'
MATT WILLIS

Stacey's one of those people who don't have a mean bone in their body. I don't either, but I don't have any bones in my body, so that's not saying very much.

It seemed like everybody knew she was going to win the show right from the start. Dom Joly said as much to her.

And as far as I'm concerned, if you're prepared to eat a kangaroo's lady bits, you deserve everything you get.

'I COULD DO SO MUCH MORE THAN I THOUGHT I COULD EVER DO. I DIDN'T THINK I COULD EVER SIT IN A ROOM WITH BUGS, LET ALONE LET THEM BE POURED ALL OVER ME. I DIDN'T THINK I COULD SLEEP OUTDOORS. I'M NOT AS RUBBISH AS I THINK.'
STACEY SOLOMON

DOUGIE POYNTER, series 11

Being in a boyband is always going to guarantee you a bunch of votes on this show. Ask Matt Willis, J from Five or even Antony Costa. But to go all the way and win still requires something a little bit special.

Dougie took jungle life in his stride. I suppose with the unsanitary conditions, terrible food and uncomfortable beds, he just felt like he was back on tour with McFly.

As far as Dougie was concerned, he had a bit of a laugh with his mates for three weeks and then got to wear a wooden crown. Good for him.

'I CAN'T BELIEVE I'VE BEEN CROWNED AN ACTUAL KING. THE FIRST LAW IS EVERYONE HAS TO BE NAKED TWENTY-FOUR SEVEN.'
DOUGIE POYNTER

'I THINK DOUGIE IS THE PERFECT JUNGLE KING.'
KERRY...

CHARLIE BROOKS,
series 12

ANT: Charlie, you are now our Queen of the Jungle. How do you feel?

CHARLIE BROOKS: Silly.

Charlie Brooks is one of the loveliest people you could hope to meet. Okay, so she pushed Barry Evans to his death in Albert Square, but we all have our moments.

It's worth remembering that Charlie managed to hold onto her temper even when she was dealing with Helen Flanagan's dramatics. For that alone she deserves some sort of award.

KIAN EGAN, series 13

'THERE'S NOTHING THAT I WON'T DO.'
KIAN EGAN

On his first day, Kian got a tick. He hadn't even made it to camp. It didn't faze him at all, though. Medic Bob came in and pulled it out. You could tell right there that he'd be able to take anything the jungle threw at him.

Becca Walker, Executive Producer

Another boyband member, another King of the Jungle. What is it with these boyband singers?

Still, you can't fault the viewers for giving Kian their votes. He was your classic jungle king: he had an absolute blast, he kept his nose out of trouble, and he blubbed a lot about missing his family.

Always a vote-winner.

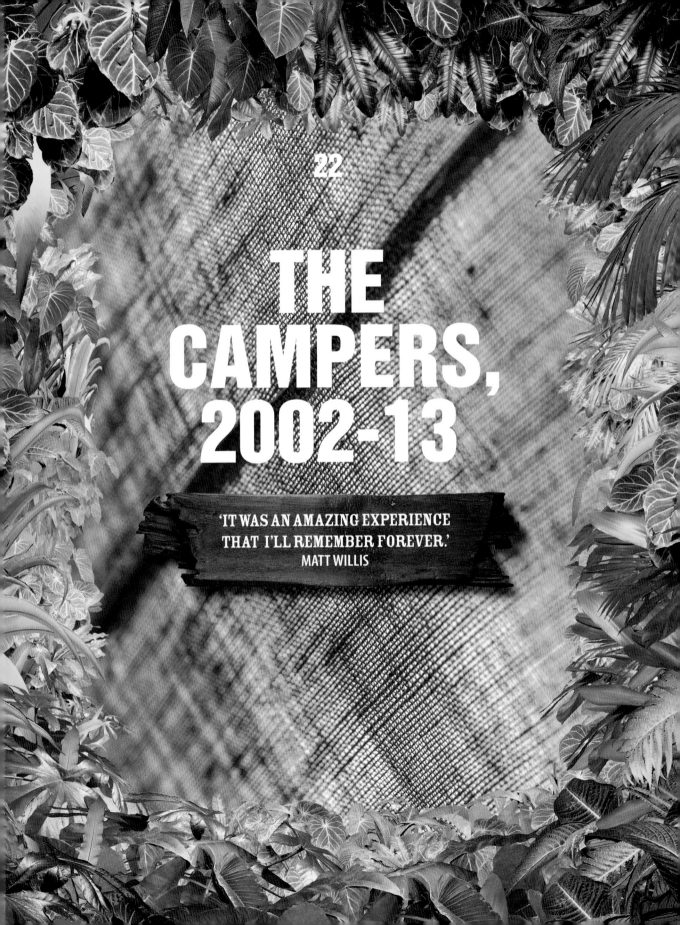

22

THE CAMPERS, 2002-13

'IT WAS AN AMAZING EXPERIENCE
THAT I'LL REMEMBER FOREVER.'
MATT WILLIS

To all the celebrities who've hopped on a plane to Australia, climbed into a chopper and flown over miles and miles of broccoli to head into the unknown –
THANK YOU.

You've entertained millions of people. You've pushed yourself to your limits.

You're all winners.*

We salute you.

Series 1, 2002

Tony Blackburn
Tara Palmer-Tomkinson
Christine Hamilton
Nell McAndrew
Rhona Cameron
Darren Day
Nigel Benn
Uri Geller

Series 2, 2003

Phil Tufnell
John Fashanu
Linda Barker
Wayne Sleep
Antony Worrall Thompson
Toyah Wilcox
Catalina Guirado
Chris Bisson
Danniella Westbrook
Sian Lloyd

Series 3, early 2004

Kerry Katona
Jennie Bond
Peter Andre
Lord Brocket
Katie Price (Jordan)
Alex Best
Neil Ruddock
John Lydon
Diane Modahl
Mike Read

Series 4, late 2004

Joe Pasquale
Paul Burrell
Fran Cosgrave
Janet Street-Porter
Sophie Anderton
Antonio Fargas
Sheila Ferguson
Vic Reeves
Nancy Sorrell
Natalie Appleton
Brian Harvey

Series 5, 2005

Carol Thatcher
Sheree Murphy
Sid Owen
Jimmy Osmond
Bobby Ball
Antony Costa
Jenny Frost
David Dickinson
Kimberley Davies
Jilly Goolden
Tommy Cannon
Elaine Lordan

Series 6, 2006

Matt Willis
Myleene Klass
Jason Donovan
David Gest
Dean Gaffney
Jan Leeming
Malandra Burrows

*That's not strictly true.

Phina Oruche
Lauren Booth
Faith Brown
Scott Henshall
Toby Anstis

Series 7, 2007

Christopher Biggins
Janice Dickinson
Jason 'J' Brown
Cerys Matthews
Gemma Atkinson
Anna Ryder Richardson
Rodney Marsh
John Burton Race
Lynne Franks
Katie Hopkins
Marc Bannerman

Series 8, 2008

Joe Swash
Martina Navratilova
George Takei
David Van Day
Simon Webbe
Nicola McLean
Brian Paddick
Esther Rantzen
Timmy Mallett
Carly Zucker
Dani Behr
Robert Kilroy-Silk

Series 9, 2009

Gino D'Acampo
Kim Woodburn

Jimmy White
Justin Ryan
Stuart Manning
Sabrina Washington
George Hamilton
Joe Bugner
Samantha Fox
Colin McAllister
Lucy Benjamin
Katie Price
Camilla Dallerup

Series 10, 2010

Stacey Solomon
Shaun Ryder
Jenny Eclair
Dom Joly
Kayla Collins
Aggro Santos
Linford Christie
Gillian McKeith
Britt Ekland
Alison Hammond
Lembit Öpik
Sheryl Gascoigne
Nigel Havers

Series 11, 2011

Dougie Poynter
Mark Wright
Fatima Whitbread
Antony Cotton
Willie Carson
Crissy Rock
Emily Scott
Jessica-Jane Clement
Lorraine Chase
Pat Sharp

Sinitta
Stefanie Powers
Freddie Starr

Series 12, 2012

Charlie Brooks
Ashley Roberts
David Haye
Eric Bristow
Hugo Taylor
Rosemary Shrager
Helen Flanagan
Colin Baker
Linda Robson
Limahl
Nadine Dorries
Brian Conley

Series 13, 2013

Kian Egan
David Emanuel
Lucy Pargeter
Joey Essex
Amy Willerton
Rebecca Adlington
Alfonso Ribeiro
Steve Davis
Matthew Wright
Vincent Simone
Laila Morse
Annabel Giles

THANK YOU FROM BRUCEY

'I LOVED EVERY SINGLE MOMENT OF IT.
I WOULD NOT HAVE MISSED IT FOR THE
WORLD AND I'D NEVER DO IT AGAIN.'
CHRISTOPHER BIGGINS

THIRTEEN YEARS! Thirteen years! Is it really thirteen years since I started doing this show? Thanks to my plastic surgeons, you wouldn't think it. And thanks to my fondness for cocktails, I can't remember much about it.

Today, *I'm A Celebrity … Get Me Out Of Here!* is as popular as ever – and that's all down to you, our loyal viewers. So I'd like to thank you from the bottom of my heart. Seriously. You've made several of my ex-wives very, very rich.

Way back at the start, a handful of people were responsible for creating *I'm A Celebrity … Get Me Out Of Here!* And I think it's only right that they get all the credit they deserve – in other words, a very small mention on the last page of the book.

They are: Jim Allen, Brent Baker, Richard Cowles, Mark Busk-Cowley, Alexander Gardiner, Stuart Morris, Will Smith and Natalka Znak.

What became of these TV geniuses? Well, a couple still work on the show. A few went off and found success elsewhere. One of them, last I heard, is living in a skip and recently swapped a kidney for a bottle of gin.

> 'WHAT A BEAUTIFUL PLACE THE JUNGLE IS. WHAT A BEAUTIFUL PLACE.'
> DEAN GAFFNEY

Finally, I'd like to say a huge thank you to the hosts of *I'm A Celebrity …
Get Me Out Of Here!*, two of the funniest, most talented and hardest-working
people in show business: Ant and Dec. Much as it pains me to admit it, there
literally would be no show without them.

I've often said to the boys that my houses, Lamborghinis and many, many
yachts belong as much to them as they do to me.

But not in any legally binding way.

I hope you've enjoyed reading my story – the story of *I'm A Celebrity …
Get Me Out Of Here!* I don't know what the future holds for me. But if it
involves as much screaming, shrieking and blind terror as the last thirteen
years, then I'll be one happy cockroach.

See you around.

Brucey

'I MISS THE JUNGLE EVERY DAY. IF A
HELICOPTER CAME HERE TO TAKE ME AWAY,
I'D CLIMB ABOARD. IT WAS JUST A MAGICAL,
MAGICAL MOMENT IN MY LIFE.'
ESTHER RANTZEN

TRANSWORLD PUBLISHERS
61–63 Uxbridge Road, London W5 5SA
A Random House Group Company
www.transworldbooks.co.uk

First published in Great Britain in 2014 by Bantam Press
an imprint of Transworld Publishers

A CIP catalogue record for this book
is available from the British Library.

ISBN 9780593073483

Addresses for Random House Group Ltd companies outside the UK
can be found at: www.randomhouse.co.uk
The Random House Group Ltd Reg. No. 954009

The Random House Group Limited supports the Forest Stewardship Council®
(FSC®), the leading international forest-certification organisation. Our books
carrying the FSC label are printed on FSC®-certified paper. FSC is the
only forest-certification scheme supported by the leading environmental
organisations, including Greenpeace. Our paper procurement policy can be
found at www.randomhouse.co.uk/environment

Photographs © ITV/Rex Features
Additional photography by Nigel Wright
Brucey Illustrations by Bill Ledger
Map on page 24 by Luke Strachan www.rooftopfox.com
Picture research: Shane Chapman and Sean James Cameron
Additional picture clearance: Jane Edyvean

Design by EnvydesignLtd

Printed and bound in Germany
2 4 6 8 10 9 7 5 3 1

MIX
Paper from
responsible sources
FSC
www.fsc.org   FSC® C011124